REJOICE

REJOICE . . . ALWAYS!

Studies in Philippians 4

JOHN GWYN-THOMAS

THE BANNER OF TRUTH TRUST

THE BANNER OF TRUTH TRUST
3 Murrayfield Road, Edinburgh EH12 6EL
PO Box 621, Carlisle, Pennsylvania 17013, USA

★

First published 1989
ISBN 0 85151 562 2

★

Typeset in 10½/12pt Linotron Plantin
At The Spartan Press Ltd, Lymington, Hants
Printed and bound in Great Britain by
BPCC Hazell Books Ltd
Member of BPCC Ltd
Aylesbury, Bucks

TO CHRISTOPHER
AND ELIZABETH

Acknowledgement

I would like to acknowledge the support which I have received from Lady Catherwood in editing these sermons. Without her initial and continuing encouragement I do not believe they would ever have been published.

Contents

Contents

John Gwyn-Thomas

Not till I was gathering material for this memoir did I learn that John, who was one of my closest friends for a quarter of a century, was a revival convert, having come to Christ at fourteen when the Spirit of God impacted his school. I never heard much from him of what his life was like before we met, for neither of us lived in the past; when we were together, we would talk about the present and the future rather than reminisce. Yet I gathered early on that he had known revival experiences, and I ought to have guessed that it was revival that produced him, since the marks of revival were so clear and strong upon him.

Revival, like regeneration, is a characteristic work of God, in the sense that, below the surface-level differences of culture and temperament that give Christians and spiritual movements their individuality, what God does at the deepest level is the same every time. Thus, in regeneration the inner self ('the hidden man of the heart,' *I Pet. 3:4, KJV*) is so changed through union with the risen Christ that the motivating dispositions of the Son's incarnate life – responsiveness to God the Father, trust in him and his word, love for the righteousness he loves and hatred for the sin he hates, a desire above all to know, worship, serve, please, honour and glorify him for all eternity, and a heart of compassion for needy people – become central to our being. These are the changes that always occur in the new birth, whoever and whatever we are by nature, and whether or not we grasp the dimensions of the change at the time when it happens.

Similarly, in revival God always comes close, so that the sense of being in his holy presence under his searching eyes becomes inescapable. (John used to say that there was a *tinc* in the air, meaning a kind of moral and spiritual electricity, at such times.) What happens then? Guilt, festering sins that pollute, moral dishonesty, spiritual rebellion against God, public pettiness and secret shame, are brought home to the conscience by God's convicting Spirit, sometimes with overwhelming force. Some feel compelled publicly to confess these things to others, in order to get them out of their own system. Unbelievers turn, and Christians return, to the Christ of Calvary in repentance and faith. A deep sense of the greatness of God, the sinfulness of sin, and the joyfulness of being saved, remains with them thereafter, indelible as a tattoo. So it was, very strikingly, with John.

This came out the first time we met. It was in October 1950, at the first evening meal of term in Wycliffe Hall, the theological college where I had studied for a year already. John, one of the new intake, was sitting opposite me, a little Welshman with a great grin and an inner gaiety and liveliness that attracted me from the start. He was clearly not old, though his hair was greying, but he seemed to display a wisdom, maturity, and all-round spiritual adulthood that set him apart. It was once said, with some awe, of the seventeen-year-old village preacher Charles Spurgeon that he was as experimental (puritan word for experiential) as if he had been a hundred years old in the faith. That was how John, the twenty-seven-year-old ordinand, was coming across to me. I asked him what he had done before entering Wycliffe. He told me, without being specific, that he had been a schoolmaster. He asked me what course I was on. I told him I was researching a Puritan, and that the Puritans had helped me enormously, particularly by enabling me to understand the mortification of sin. 'Mortification?' he said, 'Let's have a talk.' The talk followed the meal and lasted about three hours. I had learned about mortification from John Owen; John had learned about it through some unhappy experiences among his contemporaries. By the end of the evening we were fast friends.

A few months later, he and I were together on a college mission team in Bristol. I recall the authority that his preaching carried, and I recall too the meeting for Christian nurses that he and I took. Our aim was to encourage, and our strategy was to make use of our own testimony. They listened politely to twenty minutes of me; then John spoke, and with the help of questions went on for two hours. I dropped out, watched, and marvelled. The sense of proven reality that radiated from everything John said was riveting, and the nurses were riveted, just as I was. The meeting warmed up: dutiful gravity dissolved into exhilarated wonder at the graciousness of God and the magnificent possibilities of the Christian life. 'There was a *tinc* there,' said John as we staggered back to the hostel shortly before midnight. I didn't disagree.

The outward events of John's life were not spectacular, and can be quickly told. Born in 1923 in Swansea of Anglican parents, he was brought up in a happy, close-knit family. He received his schooling from the age of eleven on at the Emmanuel Grammar School affiliated to the Bible College of South Wales. At eighteen he joined the school staff as a teacher and housemaster and did both jobs while working for a London external B.A.; this he duly secured, though at the cost of much lost sleep. After a short period of national service as a mineworker, he returned to the school. There, he tasted revival again. Following these experiences he married in 1949, and began to prepare for ordained ministry.

After spending two years at Wycliffe Hall, John served three parish units. He learned his trade at Christ Church, Surbiton, where two years' apprenticeship at the parish church led on to three years (1954–57) as curate-in-charge of the daughter congregation, Emmanuel, Tolworth. While there he raised money to build a new hall, something he had been assured could not be done. (In his next parish he raised money to build a new church, another thing that he had been assured could not be done.) In 1957 he became rector of Illogan with Portreath and Trevenson, a trio of churches in West Cornwall that seemed to need a strong hand and steady teaching. It was a difficult situation, but over a period of eight years John proved there the power of the gospel to unify and reinvigorate. Then in 1965 he became vicar of St Paul's, Cambridge, where he fulfilled a stable and stabilising ministry of sowing and tending the good seed of faith, hope, love, holiness, and joy in the Lord. During those years he was noticed by the discerning as one of the wisest and most skilful Reformed pastors in England. My view, however, for what it is worth, is that at no time was he as widely known as he deserved to be.

The end came unexpectedly, in 1977, through the second of two major coronaries. John loved life and had not expected to die at fifty-four, but during his ten days in hospital before the second, fatal coronary struck him down, the medical staff found him a peaceful and relaxed patient, calm and cheerful, and grew very fond of him. His outward peace reflected peace within. 'If the Lord wants to take me, I'm willing to go,' he said to one visitor. He went early one morning, unnoticed. Nobody saw or heard him die, and I think that is how he would have wanted it: no calling of attention to himself, and no fuss. He was clear, after all, that there was nothing special about him. If you had suggested otherwise, he would have laughed. Like other Reformed saints, he was sure of his own essential unimportance; God could work just as well through others, and every time he chose to work through John Gwyn-Thomas it was truly amazing grace.

The fact is, however, that both as a didactic preacher and as a pastoral counsellor John was unusually strong, despite the inner diffidence and inferiority feelings with which he had constantly to battle. His theology was that of the

Reformers and Puritans as maintained most notably in recent times by Dr D. Martyn Lloyd-Jones (with whom John had close, friendly and fruitful ties of long standing). His method was always to teach and apply the Bible. His style, both in the pulpit and in the study, was that of the schoolmaster: not impassioned but emphatic, not rhetorical but analytical, not literary but life-centred. Living by the grace of God in Christ was his focal theme. Three stresses in particular marked all his counselling and preaching: the sinfulness of sin, the necessity of thought, and the duty of joy. Something should be said about each stress separately.

On the sinfulness of sin: John's pastoral preaching gained notice everywhere (not always favourable notice, be it said) by reason of the amount of pulpit time that he spent detecting and exposing sin. Irritation and impatience at this diet did not worry him, for he knew that invalids often dislike the taste of their medicine and would prefer not to be told what the doctor thinks is wrong with them. In the course of a wide-ranging and much valued pastoral ministry to individuals, John was used to bring to chastity several practising homosexuals whom other pastors and physicians had referred to him. I once asked him the secret of his effectiveness in doing this, insofar as he himself knew what it was. 'They have got to see that it's sin,' he replied; 'I hold them to that.' There was, no doubt, more to it than that; had John not been a relaxed man's man who walked with each struggler in what today we call an accountability relationship, I do not suppose he would have had such success. But insisting on the sinfulness of the sin was the hinge on which his entire therapy turned.

On the necessity of thought: John constantly resisted the anti-intellectual, irrational temper of our time, insisting that the life of faith is first and foremost a life of knowing and of thinking. He saw all human lapses, beginning with Eve's in Eden, as springing from the thoughtlessness that lets blind impulse take over, and he insisted that under God the cure for sins through Christ and the road to righteousness in Christ starts with a right use of the mind, meditating on biblical truth and applying it to one's own case. Those who wanted a quick fix spiritually found this teaching barren and left, but others found the diet nourishing and became increasingly human and wise in Christ through digesting it.

On the obligation of joy: it was significant that the subject John chose for his address to the 1961 Puritan and Reformed Studies Conference was *The Puritan Doctrine of Joy*. His paper celebrated the Puritan emphasis (and it was the Puritan emphasis, historically – make no mistake about that!) on rejoicing in God as a privilege, a duty, and a task and in the following sentences he spoke as much for himself as for his Puritan mentors:

> One of the controlling principles of (Puritan) preaching was 'the primacy of the intellect'. Man is a rational being, and God moves man by addressing truth to his mind. As we consider the directions given by such men as Howe, Baxter and Sibbes, we must observe their emphatic insistence that joy is the only rational state of the Christian in view of the truth about his spiritual condition (i.e., that he has been saved from the miseries of hell for the glory and joy of heaven). For Christians to lack joy is utterly irrational. The state of joy is a reasonable state: it has the best of foundations for it ultimately rests on the gracious nature and being of God. John Howe devotes a whole treatise to this subject under the title *Of Delighting in God*.[1]

And John drilled his hearers in the fine art of Christian rejoicing, just as his Puritan role-models did before him.

The sermons in this volume are typical of John's pastoral preaching. Under the title *Parochial and Plain Sermons* John Henry Newman published elegant homilies that he had

[1] *Press toward the Mark*, London: Evangelical Magazine, 1962, p. 19.

written out word for word. John Gwyn-Thomas, however, was what Richard Baxter called a 'downright' preacher rather than an elegant one, and spoke from full notes rather than a complete script. The reconstructing of the sermons for reading has been done by his widow, Nancy, who has performed her labour of love with great skill; in my mind's ear I can hear John saying just about every sentence! And these messages are eminently 'parochial and plain': they are meant for ordinary Christians who want to know how to please God and keep on the path to heaven, and they appear now, not only as a tribute to John's memory, but in the belief that their bibilical insight and their blunt, down-to-earth realism about the business of living by faith will bring a lot of help to a lot of people. I am grateful for them, and I think you will be too.

J. I. Packer
Regent College, Vancouver
August 1989

1
Stand Fast in the Lord

Therefore, my brethren, whom I love and long for, my joy and crown, stand firm thus in the Lord, my beloved. Philippians 4:1

When studying the epistles of Paul closely, it is possible to come to the conclusion that he was a dry, theologically-minded ecclesiastic. But if we read his epistles aright we see, in fact, that he was a warm-hearted pastor who had a loving concern for his flock. He said, 'My brethren, whom I love and long for, my joy and crown, my beloved.' It is very common for people to think that doctrine or teaching is rather remote or academic, but this is not true because doctrine is *basic*: it is the foundation of our Christian lives. If we are to be concerned about life and living as God wants us to live, then we must be concerned about doctrine.

That is precisely what we see in this text – it begins with the word 'therefore', and this links it to what has gone before, which is essentially doctrine, namely, our heavenly citizenship, our expectation of the coming of Christ, our bodies to be like His by the power which enables Him to subject all things to Himself. It is in the knowledge of these great doctrinal truths, therefore, that our lives should be lived, and the effect for which Paul was looking was that these Philippians should 'stand fast in the Lord' – that is the practical implication. We are no different today; our great Pastor speaks to *us* still.

Why was it necessary for Paul, as a pastor, to call upon these people in Philippi to stand fast in the Lord, and how should we see ourselves in the light of what he wrote to them? With this in mind let us look at this text more closely.

THE PASTOR'S PERSPECTIVE

If we try to see this Philippian church through the eyes of Paul we will be able to understand more fully his call to 'Stand fast in the Lord'. Let us consider it in two ways.

First, we are conscious that *he loved this church* – he called them 'my brethren'; this is the first thing he said about them, and then he said very deliberately, 'whom I love'. His heart was going out towards them; he longed to see them again. They had come to faith through him; they were not a vague body of people. This church was composed of individuals who cared about him in prison, and he was concerned to know how they were progressing in the faith. He calls them his *joy* – even in prison! We all know how much joy we get from natural things but here is the apostle talking about spiritual joy, and his joy was this church and the spiritual progress they were making. How many of us find joy in this way? He then calls them his *crown*. He may have thought of this as the crown that the Lord would give him at the last day, or that the church at Philippi was the crown as the reward for his labours. This church had come to Christ through his ministry, and he wanted them to continue in Christ. Finally, he calls them his *beloved*; indeed I do not think he loved any church more than he loved the Philippian church. Because he loved them he was concerned about them; he wanted to encourage them, to warn them, to do all he could to see that they continued as the people of God in the situation in which God had put them. He exhorts them to keep the faith so that they might be numbered among the citizens of heaven, and he sends them an exhortation in these words: 'Stand fast in the Lord.' We must realize that just as the Pastor of pastors was speaking to the church at Philippi through the apostle Paul, He is still speaking to His church today and saying to us, 'Stand fast in the Lord.'

Not only did the apostle love the Philippian church, but *he perceived their dangers*. In normal circumstances, to stand up is perfectly natural unless there is some opposition which could threaten this. You call on people to stand up only if you see that there are dangers which could knock them down. Paul could see things of which this church was unaware, or which they were taking for granted, and he felt the need to warn them; at a distance he could see their dangers more objectively. They were young in the faith and lived in a hostile and godless world. Let us remind ourselves that although the scene may have changed, and the dangers may have changed in appearance, in reality we are just as vulnerable as they were. Human nature is the same. The powers around us have changed only their shape and form, but they are basically the same. The devil is still at work, so we too face a similar situation to that which the Philippian church faced, whether we realize it or not.

What could have been tempting these Philippians or oppressing them at that time? I suggest there were three things.

1. There were *pressures from within the church*, false teachers who would have prevented them from depending on Christ alone. These doctrinal attacks were from people who said that, in addition to Jesus Christ, they also needed circumcision. They wanted to add to the gospel of Jesus Christ, saying that salvation was by works as well as through faith in Him; justification by faith alone was not sufficient. Do not let us seek to add anything to the pure gospel of Jesus Christ – lest anybody thinks he stands in the presence of God on any other ground but that Jesus Christ came into this world and died upon the cross for our salvation. We are

clothed with His perfect righteousness and nothing else; we do not need to add anything to His atoning death.

Today we find, too, that the very basis of Scripture is being attacked again, unfortunately, from within the church. The authority of the Bible is being undermined, and the historicity of Jesus Christ is being challenged. Some theologians say that we cannot know anything about the Jesus of history. They attack the very heart of the gospel when, in their arrogance and pride, they question the virgin birth and resurrection of our Lord. They seek to bring God, our Creator and Redeemer, down to the level of their own fallen understanding and the devil is quick enough to use this to shake the faith of others. The result is that the very foundations of the faith are being attacked by the confusion of man, who with his sinful mind tries to work out the gospel of Jesus Christ. It does not matter whether it is in philosophical or theological terms, as long as *it is man's opinion*. But I do not want to be on my death bed with man's opinion; I want to know the truth as it is revealed from God.

2. Then there was the subtlety of worldliness which was affecting this church at Philippi. These Christians were living where immorality and vice surrounded them and were even associated with religion; this was their culture pattern. There was gross materialism, the sin of compromise in seeking the respectability of wealth and the security of possessions. Today we have changed the word immorality into freedom, self-fulfilment, 'being yourself'; we flout morals and standards as if God had not revealed what is right and wrong. The difference between right and wrong has been undermined, and the moment we take this position we are in danger of losing sight of the God with whom we have to do – the holiness of God, the purity of God, the righteousness of God, the standards of God. In other words we have been undermined fundamentally – right in the very foundations of our society. Paul was aware of all these dangers and pressures

around the Philippian church and he told them to stand firm, to stand firm spiritually and morally, lest they adopt the viewpoint of the world and no longer live as the children of God.

3. But the apostle has yet another warning for the Philippians. They gathered together as a church; they were good, honest and upright people as they should have been, but they became contented and then self-satisfied, very respectable, very secure in what they were. They had begun to adopt the viewpoint of the world around them, that is, their ultimate source of security was in this world and its possessions. As Christians today we are just as liable to fall into the same state of mind. The devil is so subtle that before we know where we are we have come to live for these things. We become so self-satisfied that we begin to think of life in terms of our work and our pleasures, and we no longer think of life as an act of service to God. Whether we are young or old we are always the servants of Jesus Christ; we are always in a missionary situation. Paul was concerned that this church had become self-centred and indifferent to the needs of the unevangelized world around them. We too may be getting into the same situation. The deceitfulness of the human heart makes us complacent about spiritual things, relaxing our watchfulness and our zeal, thus subtly being weakened without realizing it, so that before long the pressures of the world bowl us over and we are no longer standing 'in the Lord'.

'STAND FIRM'

Why was Paul telling the Philippians to 'stand firm in the Lord'? There were several reasons and they all still apply to us today.

1. He knew their *constant vulnerability*, that there was nothing automatic about living the Christian life. They must

act consciously and deliberately as being 'in Christ' He uses a Greek word which was a positive command – 'stand firm'.

2. Amid all the pressures which come against us there must be a *conscious activity*. We must deliberately remind ourselves daily and repeatedly what we are in Christ. We are in Him; His Spirit indwells us. We have the power and the resources to live as His children. One of the dangers facing Christians is that we may not keep standing in the Lord. We are meant to help each other but, at the same time, our real standing should be 'in the Lord'.

3. Standing firm *requires an effort*; it means standing firm in *all* situations. We must *learn* to live in this way, day in and day out, that in all our circumstances we can say each morning: 'Thank You, Lord, for another day. I am Yours; help me to live as Your child today; let me be what You want me to be. Grant that Your Holy Spirit will give me grace to meet everything that comes to me today as a child of God, just as You would have lived.' The Christian faith is dynamic and it applies to everything, everybody, and every situation – to every part of our lives.

4. Standing firm may be very *costly*, especially when the opposition is strong; it may be wearying and wearing. It may even cost us our lives in order to stand. Let us be realistic – this is what is happening to Christians in other parts of the world. When they stand firm in the Lord they are put in prison, and we may be called to face the same one day.

5. It needs *courage* to be a Christian. Opposition is strong and we may get wounded in the conflict. We know that there is no temptation which will come to us but that, with the temptation, the power will be given so that we will be able to overcome, so that we might live as the children of God.

'IN THE LORD'

What does it mean to be 'in the Lord'? Although the apostle

sees these people under pressures he also sees them 'in the Lord'. Let us consider this in three ways.

1. We are 'in the Lord' because we have run to Him as a refuge, a refuge from the penalty of our sin. We have run to Jesus Christ because we have seen that in the presence of God not one of us can stand in our own merit. 'All have sinned and come short of the glory of God' (*Rom. 3:23*). But God has done something about it. He has sent His Son to die on the cross for us; He reckons to us the righteousness of Jesus Christ even as He reckoned our sin to Him on the cross, and He has given us His pledge of resurrection and eternal life. We stand in His righteousness at this very moment in the sight of God.

2. We are 'in Christ' because we want to follow in His footsteps in our daily lives. This means walking in the way that He would have walked so that His life becomes our life. We strive to be like Him so that we are examples of true sonship and His life can be seen in ours.

3. We are also 'in Christ' in a mystical union – the union that is between Christ and His church. The apostle said, 'I live; yet not I, but Christ lives in me' (*Gal. 2:20*). We are part of His body, branches of the true vine. This is the work of the Holy Spirit and this is why every Christian is indwelt by the Spirit of God. If we are Christians this is our status in Jesus Christ. When the devil comes with his temptations, telling us that we are failures etc., we must go back and say, 'I am in Jesus Christ.' This is why Paul says: Who shall separate us from the love of God which is shown in Christ Jesus our Lord? (*Rom. 8:35ff.*). He tells the Philippians this is where they are – in Christ – so they should stand firm in that.

The apostle is calling the Philippians to stand in the light of his teaching about what they are in Christ, and we are called to do the same. There is nothing else that will continue to give us peace of heart and joy in God. There is nothing else that will make us strong to serve the Lord, to take away that guilty conscience which prevents us from witnessing as we ought to witness, because we know that we are not being faithful.

The apostle looks at the church in Philippi and sees the possibility of it being attacked from so many sides, and he wants them to apply the doctrine of what they are already in Jesus Christ. The resources are there because they are the resources of our Lord and our Head, the resources of the Holy Spirit who dwells in our hearts to empower us to live as His children in this world. Through Paul, the Lord Jesus, the great Pastor, is telling us today, 'You are My beloved, you will be My joy in heaven, you will be My crown.' May He say to us when we meet Him, 'Well done, good and faithful servant, because you stood fast in Me.'

2
Differences and Heaven

I entreat Euodia and I entreat Syntyche to agree in the Lord. And I ask you also, true yokefellow, help these women, for they have laboured side by side with me in the gospel together with Clement and the rest of my fellow workers, whose names are in the book of life. Philippians 4:2–3

In these verses we are confronted with the importance of unity at a very local level, that is, between church members. This is an example of the value of a systematic teaching of Scripture because in this way, whether we like it or not, we must deal with all aspects of the Christian life. What was a problem in the life of the church at Philippi was disunity between two members. This incident shows us the way we should deal with disunity in our churches today.

THE REALISTIC ATTITUDE TO CHRISTIAN BEHAVIOUR

This passage reminds us of how realistic Christianity is and how the gospel works in a human situation. If we cannot learn how the gospel works out in *every* situation of our lives, there is something wrong with our Christianity. The church at Philippi was singularly free from false doctrine and irregular practice; no heresies or false doctrines had marred its faith, no schisms had divided its allegiance to the gospel. The division which was taking place in this church was a personal one between two women, Euodias and Syntyche. How did the apostle deal with this situation?

However much Paul loved the Philippian church he was not blind to their faults, nor did he attempt to cover them up. He had a realistic attitude towards Christian behaviour and he did not consider that these people at Philippi were perfect. It was because he was a loving pastor and brother in Christ that he was aware of their faults and, because he had a true love for these people at Philippi, he exposed their weakness so that it could be remedied. He was not afraid to point out their error any more than he was afraid to rebuke Peter when he was in error.

It is also important to recognize that *all* Christians can be at fault, and we must not attempt to defend or cover up any weakness which we find in our churches today. Christians are *not* perfect people; the church is not composed of completely sanctified and transformed members who no longer have weaknesses. Sinless perfection does not exist while we are in this world. The Bible teaches us quite clearly that Christians *will* sin: 'If any man sin, we have an advocate with the Father' (*1 John 2:1*). We all sin but when we acknowledge it, repent and turn to Jesus Christ there is forgiveness.

We are reminded here also that even mature Christians, those who have been used of God, can fall into error. The apostle says Euodia and Syntyche 'laboured side by side with me in the gospel together with Clement and the rest of my fellow workers'. They had been among the founders of the church at Philippi and had had the privilege of working with the apostle himself. They were probably both deaconesses of the church, but this was not a guarantee that they could not fall into sin. The devil attacks us all the way through life. The form of attack changes; he may not get us in one way, but he will do his best to get us in another, if not at one time then at another. We are always confronted with a subtle enemy, and watchfulness must be the order of the day.

We are not told the cause of the differences of opinion between these two women, but it is obvious that they had been quarrelling and that whatever happened had spoiled the relationship between them, broken the unity of the fellowship in the church, and brought dishonour to the name of God. Moreover, when people in the church take up different attitudes and they each have followers, it brings about a party spirit. These disputes among Christians come about usually as a result of two specific sins – parent sins, because they bring a brood of other sins with them – namely, pride and jealousy. Both these women had had an experience of God and been successful in the work of the church. But it may have been that one of them had experienced a special blessing from God, some new gift; or perhaps she had been able to adopt a successful technique in her work or been appointed to a particular office in the church. Whatever the cause, one of them had received some gift or position and probably pride had crept in. Even in the Christian life it is so easy to exalt oneself, to attach great importance to one's own experience and to try to impose this same experience on other people. We begin to think we are more worthy than others who have not had the same experience. No form of pride is so subtle and yet so damaging as spiritual pride.

On the other hand it is likely that the other woman then became jealous, and so a conflict was triggered off between the two of them. Each one held to her own opinion and refused to give way to the other. Pride and jealousy led them both into an entrenched position of stubbornness and selfishness. Their own personal viewpoint, experience or position had become more important to them than their unity in Christ and in the church. The blessing which God had given to one was misused so that both women not only displeased Him by bringing about disunity in the church, but they also brought dishonour to the name of God. *God's gifts must be used in His way*, through patience and prayer, not by force of personality or emotional appeals.

This helps us to understand the value of the Word of God, which comes with its objective teaching and begins to search our hearts, exposing the true nature of the weaknesses within us and bringing us back to the realization that it is only by God's grace that we are in the kingdom. It reminds us constantly of our need of vigilance. 'Watch and pray, lest you enter into temptation', said the Lord Jesus to His disciples. This strife and division took place in the church at Philippi, but it can also happen amongst us either on a personal level or in the church.

THE GENTLE BUT FIRM PASTOR

Because the apostle loved this church at Philippi he did not leave them on their own in this error. What did he do to help them?

He made an appeal to *both* women, quite separately: 'I entreat Euodia and I entreat Syntyche to agree in the Lord.' He did this quite deliberately because *both* of them were wrong.

But he wanted the quarrel settled spiritually. He did not want them just to patch things up superficially, because the animosity would have remained underneath. He wanted to get to the root of the trouble so that they would face up to what was dividing them and be one in the Lord. So he reminds them that the things which united them were far greater than those which divided them, that is, they were both redeemed through Jesus Christ; they both had the same heavenly Father and the indwelling of the Holy Spirit; both of them were going to dwell eternally in the presence of God. He appealed to them to examine themselves in this unifying perspective, involving their minds as well as their hearts so that they would see the triviality of natural differences in the light of this great unity in the Spirit. And secondly, he recalls their former unity in the service of Jesus Christ – 'they have laboured side by side with me in the gospel'. They had both had the privilege of working with him in the founding of the church; they had both shared in the same disciplined effort.

Every church today is composed of people with different personalities, different gifts, different points of view, etc., but we must always remind ourselves that the things which unite us are far more important and far greater than the things which divide us. Divisions within churches have caused more harm to the name of Christ than almost anything else. As Bishop Ryle wrote in his book *Holiness*, 'Love to Christ is the common meeting point of believers of every branch of Christ's church on earth . . . Calvinist or Arminian . . . Established or Free . . . About forms and ceremonies, about church government and modes of worship they often differ widely. But on one point, at any rate, they are united. They have all one common feeling towards Him on whom they build their hope of salvation. They love the Lord Jesus Christ.' The same attitude towards the essentials of the Christian faith applies to all of us today. On the other hand, the tremendous areas of doctrinal difference which divide the Protestant Church from the Church of Rome will remain unresolved until they are settled by a fundamental belief in the truth of the Word of God.

Paul was also aware that the situation between these two women had lasted too long and was affecting the life of the church, so he calls on a 'yokefellow' to come in and be of pastoral help to them: 'And I ask you also, true yokefellow, help these women.' We can learn from this example that when there are times of friction within the church, it is sometimes necessary for someone who is not involved in the situation to help us to see matters more objectively, and to see our personal disagreements in the light of our faith as a whole, to see them in relation to God. We all need one another in this life and we must be humble enough to accept advice and help. As Christians we are all members of the family of God and we need to act as a church through whom the life of Jesus Christ can flow to those around us who are in such desperate need. It is vital for us to realize that the fruit of the Spirit is not defined as holding a position in the church, being a preacher, a teacher, or even a missionary, because these positions depend upon our gifts and calling. 'The fruit of the Spirit is love, joy, peace, patience, kindness, goodness, faithfulness, gentleness, self-control . . . If we live by the Spirit, let us also walk by the Spirit' (*Gal. 5:22, 25*). *All* Christians have this calling. So for members of the church to be at variance with one another destroys them spiritually because they quench the Spirit by their actions.

THE BOOK OF LIFE

The apostle makes one more appeal to these women which is not quite so direct. He wants them to see themselves from a different standpoint. Should they be in conflict with each other when they both have their names written in the book of life? Once again he is reminding them of a great spiritual truth, which applies to *every* Christian, namely, that it does not matter how unimportant or insignificant we may appear in the eyes of the world or even the church, our names are written in the book of life. Every one of us is named individually before God; every one of us is significant to Him. Reference to the book of life is first mentioned in Moses' prayer of intercession when he asked to be blotted out of God's book if Israel was to be destroyed (*Exod. 32:32*). In Daniel 12:1 we are told that all the righteous who 'shall be found written in the book' will survive the eschatological tribulation. In Revelation 20:15 we read that 'whosoever was not found written in the book of life was cast into the lake of fire'. This brings home to us the reality of being numbered as one of God's people, not just during time but for eternity. *In the end the only thing that will matter is that our names are in that book of life.* Whatever position we may hold in this world, academically, socially, politically or financially, at the moment of death it will have gone; only our life with God will remain because our relationship with Him is everlasting.

As citizens of the heavenly kingdom we are to be living God's life on earth, we are to act as citizens of that kingdom. Our life is not primarily to be a constant struggle for positions in this world or even in the church, but we are to know the fullness of the life of God which is eternal. Euodia and Syntyche may have been seeking recognition or position in the church at Philippi, but when God says to us, 'I have called you by name; you are mine' – *this is to be our security and joy*. If we live this life in the light of eternity the trivial things of time are put into the right perspective. Do we live in division with the people of God? Are we seeking self-exaltation in this life only or do we live daily as those people whose names are written in the book of life? Let each one of us pray earnestly that God will enable us to live in this way so that we may shine as lights in the world.

3
Rejoicing – As a Duty (1)

Rejoice in the Lord always; again I will say, Rejoice.
Philippians 4:4

We have seen how Paul had written to the Philippians concerning the quarrel between Euodia and Syntyche and urged them to deal with this matter spiritually, and to remember that what really mattered was that their names were written in the book of life. His spirit is now lifted up to burst out with this command to the Philippian church as a whole to 'rejoice in the Lord always'. Are we really to believe that he meant the Philippians to rejoice in the Lord *always*? Is it true that he expected fallible human beings like you and me to rejoice in the Lord always, or do we rationalize our failure to do so by thinking that the apostle was somebody rather special? Let us remember that he was also a human being; he had exactly the same feelings as everybody else. He wrote this to the Philippian church because he *did not* think that this applied *only* to himself; it applied to them also and it applies to us today too.

Moreover, this was not just a passing thought in the apostle's mind; it weaves its way through this letter like a golden thread. Time and time again he mentions these words 'rejoice' and 'joy'; 'Christ is proclaimed; and in that I rejoice. Yes, and I shall rejoice' (*1:18–19*); 'I have thought it necessary to send to you Epaphroditus my brother and fellow worker . . . that you may rejoice at seeing him again' (*2:25, 28*); 'I rejoice in the Lord greatly' (*4:10*). Here the apostle is in prison, in chains and under threat of execution, but he could rejoice, and he wants the Philippians to rejoice; so there is no excuse for us!

THE DUTY OF REJOICING

The first thing that strikes us about this text is that rejoicing is laid upon us as a command; it is a duty. What Paul says is an imperative – 'rejoice'. But how can this be a duty when rejoicing involves feeling? How can we rejoice when we do not *feel* like rejoicing? How can we control our feelings? This raises the question of the relationship of our feelings to grace and to our Christian life as a whole. In considering this there are several points to be borne in mind.

As Christians, unless we refuse to allow our feelings to dominate us we are in trouble because, although they can make us very happy, they can also make us utterly miserable and, if we rely on them, we have to admit that we are completely at the mercy of our unpredictable drives and impulses. To accept this concept as being right we have to accept the consequences. Firstly, we have to deny that man is a rational being and that our feelings should normally be governed by reason. There are times when we are confronted by a problem and if we obeyed our feelings we would run away from it. There are occasions when we do not feel like doing our Christian duty or being Christ-like. Even the Lord Jesus had a battle in the garden of Gethsemane; He was weighed down when He said, 'Father, if thou art willing, remove this cup from me; nevertheless not my will, but thine, be done.' Instead of giving in to His feelings, He bowed to His Father's will. Secondly, if we all gave in to our feelings there would be chaos; we could not live together. There would be no restraint in society. Would we be prepared to accept that a rapist or a murderer should be allowed to say in court, 'I just *felt* like doing it'? No one would defend that attitude; everybody would condemn it and say that such people must control their feelings. So it is quite clear that basically our feelings cannot be allowed to govern our lives. However, to a lesser extent, the majority of us *do* allow our feelings to affect our lives. What we must realize is that our feelings are part of our personalities and in many ways we must thank God for them; life would be terrible without them. There are many feelings which are right and God-given, but we must not be ruled by them. On the other hand, some feelings may be wrong but they are not sin – only giving in to them constitutes sin. Because they are part of our personalities they too are affected by the fall; they too can be governed by the sinful natures within us. That is why we often love the things we should not love and we do not love the things we ought to love. Our feelings are perverted as much as our minds are perverted and our wills are weakened.

It is very important to remember that one of the great purposes of God in the new birth and sanctification is to restore our feelings to their proper place in our lives, so that they are governed by the will of God and not by whims or emotions which overtake us in so many different ways and at different times. Some of the feelings which we should be seeking are the outcome of the fruit of the Spirit – love, joy, peace, long-suffering, and so on. These are feelings which come to us as the direct work of the Spirit within us and, as Christians, we should be allowing the Spirit to make such changes in us – that is to change our fallen feelings into those of the fruit of the Spirit.

However much we may try to rationalize our lack of feelings in spiritual matters, we have to admit that, without question, it is our duty as members of the family of God to 'rejoice in the Lord *always*'. God has given us many duties. For example, He has said, 'Seek ye first the kingdom of God and all these things shall be added unto you'; 'Do not be anxious about tomorrow'; 'Love your enemies and pray for those who persecute you'; 'Take the log out of your own eye and then you will see clearly to take the speck out of your brother's eye'. These are some of the duties which we might find irksome, but this duty of rejoicing is what Spurgeon called a 'delightful duty'. We are called upon to be those people who are obviously enjoying life in Christ. We are not meant to be murmurers, complainers or constant grumblers. We are supposed to be rejoicing in the Lord; we cannot rejoice too much. As we seek to obey His other commands, let us apply this one to ourselves as well.

To rejoice is not only a delight which God wants us to enjoy, but it is also an example to others. When people see us in all kinds of adverse circumstances and difficulties, and yet we have joy and peace and a rejoicing of spirit, they want to know the source of this joy. From whence does it come? Our lives are attractive lives. This is a very important way of witnessing for the Lord Jesus Christ to those with whom we come into contact. Perhaps it is one of the reasons why we as Christians do not have nearly as much influence in this world as we ought to have. Too often we have not been seen to be rejoicing; we have been sombre and worried, without any peace in our lives. This spirit of rejoicing has a great effect on ourselves as well. The Bible tells us, 'The joy of the Lord is your strength.' When a Christian person is full of joy and peace, he or she is active, keen and full of zest for God and the things of God. As Spurgeon said, 'Holy joy will oil the wheels of your life's machine.' Rejoicing is an integral part of the work of the Holy Spirit within us.

GROUNDS FOR REJOICING

When we are told to rejoice in the Lord this is not something artificial; it is not something which we are stirring up within ourselves or each other. There are various ways of stirring up our feelings, and such psychological techniques are well known. But that is not what this text means. This rejoicing stems entirely from our union with Christ. There were no natural means to stir up the feelings of Paul when he was in prison awaiting execution, yet he was full of joy, 'rejoicing in the Lord'. The apostle was saying that our joy stems entirely from our union with the Lord Jesus Christ; it is *His joy* which possesses our spirits. *If we look for happiness we will never find it; if we keep searching for joy we will never attain it; but when our relationship with the Lord Jesus is right the result will be joy and peace in Him.* What effect will this joy and peace have in our lives?

In the first place, we will find that the Lord Jesus Himself is the object of our joy. We will begin to relate to Him because of what He has done for us. More and more we will begin to understand that He loves us with a depth of love which is indescribable and which can only be brought home to us by the realization of what His death on the cross means to each of us – *that* is how much He loves us. It is through His death that He is able to give us His new life in our hearts.

But behind the sacrifice of Christ's death upon the cross there is our loving and faithful heavenly Father who 'so loved the world that he gave his only begotten Son, that whosoever believeth in him should not perish but have everlasting life'. Moreover, He has chosen us to be His people. 'Blessed be the God and Father of our Lord Jesus Christ, who has blessed us in Christ with every spiritual blessing in the heavenly places, even as he chose us in him before the foundation of the world, that we should be holy and blameless before him' (*Eph. 1:3–4*).

There is also the promise of the indwelling of the Holy Spirit. He brings His life into our lives; He is the source of the power of our spiritual growth and it is only because He indwells us that we are given victory over sin in our lives and we are conformed to the image of Jesus Christ.

These are the basic grounds for our rejoicing which even the devil can never take away from us. *They are the spiritual and eternal truths – the great unchangeables.* As much as a branch is in the vine, so each one of us is in Christ. He has told us that as much as a bridegroom loves his bride, so Christ loves us, and there is not a closer union than this.

Secondly, the eternal, the everlasting and the almighty God has broken into our lives in time. He has dealt with our past and forgiven our sin because of the sacrifice of Jesus Christ on the cross. He has brought us into a relationship with Himself which is ever-present so that we can always call God our Father. He has made us citizens of His kingdom, and the secret of belonging to that kingdom lies in belonging to Him. When we look into the future, He says that He will always be our Father, and when the end of life comes He will take us to be with Himself eternally. 'I am sure that he who began a good work in you will bring it to completion at the day of Jesus Christ' (*Phil. 1:6*). There is no question about it; we are His and we shall be His for ever.

Thirdly, at the back of all our minds there is the problem of our material and physical well-being. But God has pledged Himself to take care of these things too, because the Bible tells us, 'Seek ye first the kingdom of God . . . and all these things will be added unto you' (*Matt. 6:33*). In Philippians 4:6 we are told, '*Have no anxiety about anything*'. The grounds for our joy and peace is our sonship through Christ. God tells us that He is going to deal with us in life – *in all the affairs of life* – as a beloved Father deals with a beloved son who has been cleansed by the blood of the Lord Jesus Christ and indwelt by the Holy Spirit. If anybody is reading this who is not a Christian, do you see what you are missing? Do you see the greatness of what the gospel offers you and the tragedy of being outside such a love?

CONTINUOUS REJOICING

The ground of our Christian rejoicing is entirely founded on the work of God the Father, God the Son, and God the Holy Spirit. His commitment of Himself to us in promises governs the past, the present, and the future and includes everything that we need in life, so it is quite consistent for Paul not only to say, 'Rejoice in the Lord', but 'Rejoice in the Lord *always*; again I will say, Rejoice'. His words are quite emphatic: our rejoicing is never to cease; it is to be daily, monthly and yearly, even hourly. Immediately our troubles spring to our minds. What about bereavements? They are sometimes tragic and unexpected. What about sickness, suffering and the travails of old age? These things are all very real. What about disappointments, economic uncertainties, temptations, loneliness, unemployment, weakness and sins? What about political troubles – the state of our own country and the world, tensions between nations, the threat of nuclear war, and so on? There is only one answer to these.

The starting point is that the rejoicing about which Paul was writing was to be independent of the circumstances in which he found himself. It is true that he shed tears, he knew pain, he had spent a day and a night in the sea, he suffered because he had been lashed and still bore the scars on his back; he knew the turmoil of Rome governed by Nero. He was living in a Roman world where nine out of ten people were slaves. He had all the cares of the churches upon him, opposition from the Jews and the Romans, and he was facing death. So how did he rejoice? The answer is that *he kept his eyes on the unchangeables*. God cannot change, the blood of Jesus Christ never loses its power, and the Holy Spirit will never be taken away from us, even though at times we may grieve Him. God committed Himself to us when He promised us that 'All things work together for good to them that love God, to them who are the called according to his purpose' (*Rom. 8:28*). *The Christian believes that the tiller of the craft of his life is in the hands of God*. His will is going to be done in each one of us and His will is always best. What we must do is learn to trust Him *always*.

OUR FAILURES

There are a number of failures which prevent us from rejoicing.

1. We do not really believe in the great truths about our union with the Lord Jesus Christ and all that it entails. We need to hear these truths about God continually expounded to us. We must remind ourselves that self-pity feeds on unbelief, and when we blame our circumstances or other people for our lack of joy this is tantamount to saying that God is not in control of our lives, that He does not order the lives of *all* His children *all* the time. Unbelief is the major cause of this condition.

2. Then there is our lack of discipline. We should consciously and deliberately remind ourselves daily of the great things that God has done for us. We do not discipline ourselves to make a constant use of the means of grace by reading God's word, by worship and fellowship with other Christians. Professor Keri Evans, writing about the Welsh Revival of 1904, admitted that the love of many who professed conversion during the revival grew cold because there had been a lack of insistence upon preaching during the revival.[1] There is no substitute for the sustained and comprehensive presentation of God's truth, and God rules His church *by His word and Spirit*. We should begin the day with the concept that this is *His* day and that everything that happens in it is going to work together for our good because of Jesus Christ. Unless we do that we start off wrongly. It

[1]Cited in Eifion Evans, *The Welsh Revival of 1904* (Bridgend: Evangelical Press of Wales, 1969), p. 183.

must be a continual challenge to us that throughout each day we should relate *every* circumstance in our lives to Him.

3. At times, we are disobedient to God. We do not always follow His precepts and example; we have divided loyalties and these, of course, bring estrangement between God and ourselves, and we lose our peace and joy.

4. Sometimes, when difficulties come, we turn to sources other than God. We become disheartened and begin to think we need new experiences, either spiritual or natural, as though they could lift our spirits! They may do so temporarily – but only temporarily. What we ought to do is to realize this and to rejoice in Jesus Christ. *Happiness and joy are by-products of living in union with Him.*

5. We look into the future and worry about what may or may not happen to us or to our loved ones. We do this despite the promise that the man of God 'shall not be afraid of evil tidings: his heart is fixed, trusting in the Lord' (*Ps. 112:7*). Whatever the future holds, as Christians we must believe that suffering, whether trouble or persecution, is permitted by our heavenly Father so that we may be spiritually blessed.

We have considered enough of our weaknesses to enable us to examine ourselves before God. Paul knew that this message was going to be a challenge to the Philippian church. How could Euodia and Syntyche rejoice if they were quarrelling? *When everything else is taken from us, when we cannot rejoice in anybody or anything else, we can rejoice in God.* But God has given us so many things in which we can rejoice – peace, freedom, the Bible, churches and homes, families and good health, sufficient food, and so many other things which we should actively enjoy and which we often take for granted until we lose them. We *ought* to be rejoicing. This is a present imperative – 'Rejoice in the Lord always'. Let us begin *now* to rejoice. In the mercy of God may this great servant of Christ – the apostle Paul – be to us a guide, an example, a teacher and an encourager to rejoice in the Lord. Let us take this verse seriously and live daily as those who have found a great salvation in Jesus Christ, who is a cause of unspeakable rejoicing for all of us.

4
Rejoicing – As a Duty (2)

Rejoice in the Lord always; again I will say, Rejoice.
Philippians 4:4

In the first sermon on this text I emphasized the duty of rejoicing that Paul set before the Philippian church – the duty of rejoicing *continually* – and I suggested some reasons why we fail to do this: unbelief, too much dependence on others, disobedience, and so on. I was aware, however, that I had not dealt in as much detail as necessary on the *way* in which God brings about these changes in us. *How does God change our feelings*? In this sermon I am coming down to the very practical – exceedingly practical – matter of how this can actually come about in our lives, because it is very difficult to rejoice when you are depressed or under pressure.

THE FACTS ABOUT REJOICING

I want to begin by reminding you that we all rationalize our reasons for not rejoicing. We have all got excuses which we make to ourselves and to others to account for our depressed or discouraged condition. So the first and most important point in dealing with any spiritual problem is to examine these excuses for our failure, in one way or another, to rejoice in the Lord. I call this breaking down rationalizations, and I do this when dealing with people personally. It is vitally important to do so, and I want to put before you some facts about Christians in trouble.

1. We may excuse ourselves by saying that our feelings are beyond our own control, that they are controlled by a particular type of temperament or are a direct result of adverse circumstances. To a certain extent this is true, but the feelings which are a result of our temperament or circumstances are not meant to overwhelm us and be in complete command of our feelings. The grace of the Lord Jesus Christ can give us the power to overcome the weakness of our temperament and enable us to have peace and joy irrespective of our circumstances.

2. Paul was writing to the Philippian church, which was composed of all kinds of people. Nine out of ten people you would have met in a Roman street would have been slaves; therefore, it was very possible that a large percentage of the people in this church would have been slaves. They had no rights – in fact, they had worse treatment than we give to animals in our society. For most of these people life was not a bed of roses but an exceedingly hard life of bondage.

3. The apostle did not only expect the people in this church to hear these words and apply them to themselves, but he also applied them to himself. As I have said before, *he* was in a Roman prison, isolated and awaiting a death sentence. Moreover, if you look at the book of Acts you will see that he was always rejoicing: 'And when they had inflicted many blows upon them, they threw them into prison, charging the jailer to keep them safely . . . But about midnight Paul and Silas were praying and singing hymns to God' (*Acts 16:23–25*). In Colossians 1:24 he says, 'Now I rejoice in my sufferings for your sake'; and in Philippians 4:10 he says, 'I rejoice in the Lord greatly that now at length you have revived your concern for me.'

4. In any part of the Scriptures you will find this problem

of being at peace and rejoicing in all circumstances being dealt with by God. In Genesis 32:6–7 we see Jacob faced with fear: 'And the messengers returned to Jacob, saying, "We came to your brother Esau, and he is coming to meet you, and four hundred men with him." Then Jacob was greatly afraid and distressed; and he divided the people that were with him, and the flocks and herds and camels, into two companies, thinking, "If Esau comes to the one company and destroys it, then the company which is left will escape."' In the end – as we shall see later – he came to a place of rest and peace in God, where he knew that he was perfectly secure (*verses 9–12*). David was hounded by Saul and yet he could compose Psalm 27: 'The Lord is my light and my salvation; whom shall I fear? The Lord is the stronghold of my life; of whom shall I be afraid?' Job in all his troubles said, 'Though he slay me, yet will I trust in him' (*Job 13:15*). In Acts we read of Stephen's suffering and the way in which he triumphed over it: 'But he [Stephen], full of the Holy Spirit, gazed into heaven and saw the glory of God, and Jesus standing at the right hand of God' (*Acts 7:55*). Peter wrote to the Christians in exile who were suffering: 'In this you rejoice, though now for a little while you may have to suffer various trials, so that the genuineness of your faith, more precious than gold which though perishable is tested by fire, may redound to praise and glory and honour at the revelation of Jesus Christ. Without having seen him you love him; though you do not now see him you believe in him and rejoice with unutterable and exalted joy' (*1 Pet. 1:6–8*).

5. If we look at church history from the time of the early Christians down to the present day we find the witness of people who have suffered persecution. I read recently of a Russian woman who had been in a Siberian prison for a year, and whose situation was worse than anything we could imagine; yet despite her suffering – the solitude, separation, cold and brutality – her description of that year was that it

had been her 'year of joy'. She is, in a sense, a modern martyr because she could well be killed for what she believes. These people have testified that in all different kinds of circumstances and amidst all sorts of persecutions, including violent deaths, *some peace and joy of God* has taken hold of them which they could not explain. In addition, there have been people on beds of sickness, people who have lived in abject poverty, who have had untold bereavements and sorrows, who have yet found a peace and joy in God that has been a blessing, not only to themselves, but to all those around them.

I have mentioned these points in detail once again so that we do not dismiss this as something which does not apply to us as ordinary members of the Christian church today, or think to defend ourselves by saying that these were special people – élite people, who were different from us. This letter was written to the Philippian church *in general* and it applied to all of them as it applies to all of us today. Moreover, our Lord, before He died – and, after all, He is our supreme example – expressly tells us that this peace and joy *should be ours*: 'So you have sorrow now, but I will see you again and your hearts will rejoice, and no one will take your joy from you' (*John 16:22*). No one will take your joy from you, *not one*. 'I have said this to you, that in me you may have peace. In the world you have tribulation; but be of good cheer, I have overcome the world' (*verse 33*). So whatever the world may do to us, our Lord is saying, in effect, that the peace which He gives *must be greater*. As Matthew Henry wrote: 'There is enough in God to furnish us with joy in the worst circumstances on earth.'

REJOICING IN TRIBULATION

The question is, *how* does this come about? The simplest way for me to deal with this is to remind you of Romans 5:1–5. In the first two verses of that chapter there are some clues which help us to see how this rejoicing can come about. 'Therefore, since we are justified by faith, we have peace with God through our Lord Jesus Christ. Through him we have obtained access to this grace in which we stand, and we rejoice in our hope of sharing the glory of God.' In these verses we are reminded of the greatness of what has happened to us in Christ; we have found peace with God through our Lord Jesus Christ and *we are meant to keep that peace daily*. Then in verse 3 we read: 'More than that, we rejoice in our sufferings, knowing that suffering produces endurance, and endurance produces character, and character produces hope, and hope does not disappoint us, because God's love has been poured into our hearts through the Holy Spirit which has been given to us.' This verse is a very great challenge to us all but let us be quite clear about several things before going any further.

1. As we saw in the previous chapter, *Christians have never been promised exemption from suffering* or that life would be easy for them. The Lord Jesus said, 'If any man be my disciple . . . let him take up his cross daily and follow me'; 'In the world you have tribulation.' So there is no reason for us to think that when we become Christians everything is going to be easy. The life of the apostle Paul and others in the New Testament should have shown us quite clearly that God has never promised us that we are going to be exempt from suffering in any way. Even after his call and anointing as king, David was hunted by Saul. Jeremiah, the man who was so faithful to God in his day and generation, suffered all kinds of indignities and in the end they put him in a pit to get rid of him. In 2 Corinthians 11:23–28 we read of the sufferings of Paul himself as a Christian, the way he was beaten and attacked from all quarters. It was when John was in exile in Patmos that God gave him his revelation. So let us not have any illusions about what Christianity promises us. Let me

repeat – it does not promise exemption from any sufferings. Do not let us have false expectations of a life without them.

2. Moreover, we must not automatically have a sense of guilt if we do experience tribulation, and think that it is necessarily a direct result of our own sin. We live in a fallen world and the very ways that we think and live are antagonistic to it. If the world does not criticize us at all we may be in a dangerous position. It could be that because we are such half-hearted Christians, the difference between us and non-Christians is so small that they have never even noticed we are Christians at all! Usually we find that because Christians are to be the salt of the earth, a city set upon a hill that cannot be hid, and a light that shines out into the darkness, the darkness *will* attack it. All the time, in every way, the devil will seek to attack Christians so that their lives do not reflect the light and love of God towards all mankind. So do not be surprised if you are attacked; worry if you are not attacked!

3. We must remember too that we are not fools, or as Dr Lloyd-Jones said, 'psychological oddities', in that we *seek* suffering. We are not so foolish as to do that because suffering *hurts* – 'No chastening for the present seemeth to be joyous, but grievous' (*Heb. 12:11*). Suffering *is* painful. Jacob *was* worried on the night he heard that his brother was on the way to meet him; that was why he made so many preparations for his safety. When they lashed Paul's back it hurt him, just as it would hurt us if we were lashed. Do not let us imagine that we are going to *enjoy* suffering as though we are different from everyone else. Our reactions to grief and suffering are exactly the same as those of all other human beings.

4. But the difference between us and the non-Christian is what happens then. Anybody could have been in Jacob's position, fearing desperately for his family and himself; this was a natural reaction, but if Jacob had remained in that fear

we could ask what had happened to his relationship with God. *It is when a Christian remains in a position of overwhelming grief and despondency that we need to be concerned*. There *are* various ways and means that God has given in order to help us so that our suffering does not turn into anger or bitterness or cause us to live in continual unhappiness. There *is* a place to which He can bring us where we can be at peace and rejoice, not in spite of our sufferings, but *in* our sufferings. The answer is that we have the knowledge whereby God has shown us that suffering yields the 'peaceable fruit of righteousness to those who have been trained by it' (*Heb. 12:11*). This word 'trained' or 'worked' implies a process. *This* is the key to the situation because in the suffering there is a process taking place. It would be easy to say that the Christian in suffering only needs another experience or blessing, or that he or she has only to adopt various attitudes and enthusiasms. We can be carried away by this idea, but Christianity is not like instant coffee which can be made in two minutes. When Paul uses the words 'trains' or 'produces', they imply that *there is a relationship between God and us which involves time, application, perseverance and development and which, ultimately, will result in growth*. It is not just a stoical attitude, although that is commendable in many ways. This growth is something which is going to affect our whole personality so that our attitudes and feelings are changed. In Romans 5:1–2 we read that as a consequence of our justification by faith we are accounted as righteous in the sight of God through the blood of Jesus Christ. Because we are cleansed and clothed with *His* righteousness we have hope of sharing the glory of God eternally. *This* is our destiny. We are people who know that we are justified by faith; a genuine conversion has happened to us in Christ. 'For God so loved the world that he gave his only Son, that whoever believes in him should not perish but have eternal life' (*John 3:16*). It is because of *who God is*, because of His promises, because He has revealed to us what the cross of Jesus Christ means to us in our own lives, that we see all our sufferings in the light of the cross. So when we find ourselves in any suffering there are certain things that we *know*. We know that God is love and that *He loves us as individuals*, as His own children. Paul reminds us of the character of our heavenly Father who, out of His great love for us, appoints our trials: 'Ye have forgotten the exhortation which speaketh unto you as unto children, My son, despise not thou the chastening of the Lord, nor faint when thou art rebuked of him: for whom the Lord loveth he chasteneth, and scourgeth every son whom he receiveth. If ye endure chastening, God dealeth with you as with sons; for what son is he whom the father chasteneth not?' (*Heb. 12:5–7*). In this text the apostle is saying that *we know that God is in our suffering*. He has appointed it for us within a covenant love and He is using it in a creative way in order to fulfil His great eternal purpose for us. So let us look in more detail at the ways in which suffering changes us – our attitudes and feelings. In Romans 5:3–5 we read, 'We rejoice in our sufferings, knowing that suffering produces endurance, and endurance produces character, and character produces hope, and hope does not disappoint us, because God's love has been poured into our hearts through the Holy Spirit which has been given to us.' Let us look at these points one by one.

(a) In the first place suffering produces *endurance*. The apostle means that when these pressures come and we find ourselves struggling, they expose our weaknesses; we did not realize that they were as great as this. We thought we had the faith to cope with them but suddenly we find we have not. We see ourselves as we truly are in the sight of God. That is why the apostle says, 'In me dwelleth no good thing' (*Rom. 7:18*). We become aware that there is something missing; our feelings are not what they ought to be, our faith is not what it ought to be. There is resentment, anger, bitterness and an unwillingness to accept the will of God. We find that we do not love God as much as we thought we did. We cannot cope on our own; we need the grace and strength of Christ to help us. So what do we do? *We must go back to God*, as Jacob did; we must go back to the Bible and prayer. Jacob fell on his knees before God and said, 'O God of my father Abraham and God of my father Isaac, O Lord who didst say to me, "Return to your country and to your kindred, and I will do you good" . . . Deliver me, I pray thee, from the hand of my brother, from the hand of Esau, for I fear him, lest he come and slay us all . . . But thou didst say, "I will do you good, and make your descendants as the sand of the sea, which cannot be numbered for multitude"' (*Gen. 32:11–12*). Jacob went back to the God of the covenant, and *we must go back to the God who met us in Christ*. We must genuinely seek to know God, His holiness, His love for each one of us, His sovereignty, His faithfulness – His whole character – and we learn this from the reading of His word and in prayer. We must go back to the cross and see God there in Jesus Christ, making Him 'to be sin for us, who knew no sin; that we might be made the righteousness of God in Christ' (*2 Cor. 5:21*). This is faith in action – *it is a personal application to the source of help – Jesus Christ Himself*. Because we are being taught by God how to deal with the rough passages of life in the light of the cross, we find the endurance to go on. We see the Lord Jesus afresh, we get new strength, new grace from Him in order to go through because He went through. That is why the apostle says that God told him, 'My grace is sufficient for you, for my strength is made perfect in weakness' (*2 Cor. 12:9*). He said, 'It is not me, it is Christ living in me.' This is what it means to *know* the work of the Holy Spirit within us. This experience we have had gives us greater assurance; we are stronger, clearer in our knowledge of Christ in a very practical way, and the living Lord is a reality in our lives. This is what James meant when he said, 'Blessed is the man who endures trial' (*James 1:12*); and Peter said that 'the trial of your faith' is 'much more precious than of gold' (*1 Pet. 1:7*). So when we have this experience we *know* that we are genuine Christians and not like those who are described in the parable of the sower as those who perished, those who fell by the wayside.

(b) We rejoice in suffering because suffering produces endurance and endurance produces *character*. One commentator says it is the term used for a veteran soldier as opposed to a raw recruit. So what has happened to us? This experience has given us the character of the veteran soldier who has gone through many battles, as opposed to the raw recruit who has not been in any. The veteran has already proved in the past the way that his leader can protect him in battle; he has gained strength through experience. We can go back over things in our lives and know that we have had this experience about which the apostle is speaking. We are not just talking theoretically; we know this work of God in our lives, whereby the Holy Spirit within us is daily taking us through trials and temptations so that gradually we become more like Jesus Christ.

(c) Paul says that this suffering produces endurance, endurance produces character, and character produces *hope*: our hope is strengthened. We are God's people; He is dealing with us as sons and daughters, teaching us to depend on Him and to experience His life in us as His children. We can look back and *know* that as God was faithful to us in the past, He will be faithful to us in the future. Hope does not disappoint us; our experience confirms God's word, God's care and God's grace. 'Hope does not disappoint us, because God's love has been poured into our hearts through the Holy Spirit which has been given to us' (*Rom. 5:5*). It is the fulfilment of 1 Peter 4:12 'Beloved, do not be surprised at the fiery ordeal which comes upon you to prove you, as though something strange were happening to you.' We realize a new need of our

Lord. This is a working out in faith of what has happened to us in our new birth. It is perfectly reasonable; we can follow it with our minds. We can bring our sufferings and trials before God in prayer and it *does* work; it gives us some insight into God's way of becoming more real to us and in dealing with our sinful natures – it is one of God's chief ways of enabling us to share His holiness. 'He disciplines us for our good, that we may share his holiness. For the moment all discipline seems painful rather than pleasant; later it yields the peaceful fruit of righteousness to those who have been trained by it' (*Heb. 12:10–11*). Therefore, *we have grounds for rejoicing*. More than that, if God has been faithful to us in all these things *now* we have but tasted of what He has in store for us eternally. In a very practical way God deals with man and changes him as He begins to teach him the implications of what it means to be saved by Jesus Christ. In a sense, Paul is reasoning that what God has done on the cross needs to be preached all along the line so that we come to realize and experience its full implication. It is not just one experience of God, it is to be a continual one in the daily life of every Christian. Paul sums it up when he says if God 'spared not his own Son, but delivered him up for us all, how shall he not with him also freely give us all things?' (*Rom. 8:32*). If God has given us the highest, which is His Son, if He has given us forgiveness and eternal life, everything else less than that must also be within His love to give us. This is the working out in faith of what has happened to us in the new birth. This is reasonable, rational and intelligent; it fits together, and God brings His word home to our hearts.

(d) Then the apostle goes on to say one more thing: 'Hope does not disappoint us, because God's love has been poured into our hearts through the Holy Spirit which has been given to us' (*Rom. 5:5*). He was not talking here of our love towards God but of His love towards us, a consciousness that the love of God towards us has been poured into our hearts, which are the very centre of our personalities, the centre of our beings. Our wills and our feelings will be flooded with the love of God. This is not just the working out of the implications of our faith, it is not the result of a process of training; this is something which is added directly by God through the Holy Spirit, something supernatural which God himself gives us. The realization of such love of God lifts us above our circumstances so that amid them we are filled with a sense of being His, in His loving care, with His joy and peace. God gives us an assurance so that our hearts are full to overflowing with the consciousness of His love and what He has done for us. I believe that this is what the apostle was talking about. You may say that you have not experienced this, but it may be that you have not been in the same state as Jacob was, that when it came to the test you did not go back to God and say, 'Lord, please come and meet me afresh. I *need* you.' Do not let God go until He blesses you. The Lord Jesus said He would manifest Himself to His disciples and He did so, time and time again. This is an ongoing life and God will deal with you and me as His children. You will be assured that it is God who is dealing with you and changing you, and the consciousness of His love will transcend the troubles that have beset you so that you see them from the standpoint of God. I am not giving this to you in psychological terms, but I am telling you the way that Paul explains it to us, and I have known something of this in my own experience. I think we need to take the fact of the indwelling of the Holy Spirit in the heart of every Christian very seriously and it may be that we have not done this enough. We have looked to other sources, we have tried other ways, whereas *God has blessed us in Christ*. What we need to do is to face God with His promises as Jacob did and say, 'Lord, You promised all these blessings to me; please fulfil Your promises now.' So I suggest to you that, in the words of Dr Lloyd-Jones, we need to 'sue' God to fulfil His promises, to take the indwelling of the Holy Spirit as a reality, to stand in front of these promises which are here in this text and say to God, '*I* cannot do it. You must come and meet me afresh. You must open my eyes to see again the great things that You have done for me.' He may even give you a glimpse into that eternal realm so that the joys of heaven become so great that 'the things of earth become strangely dim, in the light of His glory and grace'.

May God help us to realize the truth of the things we claim have happened to us in Jesus Christ. They are as real as God is, and here is the apostle setting them in front of himself and writing to this Philippian church to tell them, 'Rejoice in the Lord always; again I will say, Rejoice.' May God help us all to rejoice in our great God, our Saviour Jesus Christ, and in the indwelling of the Holy Spirit so that the good work that He has begun in us will continue until the day of Jesus Christ.

5
Let Your Forbearance Be Known

Let all men know your forbearance. The Lord is at hand.
Philippians 4:5

Let us thank God that we exist for Him and because of Him and that we mean so much to Him individually and personally. That itself may seem a great statement when you think of the universe, the millions of men and women who have lived, who will live, and who are living now. And yet in various ways God *has* conveyed to us that as individuals we have a great significance for Him. You remember the parable that the Lord Jesus spoke to His disciples in which He said that 'there is joy in the presence of the angels of God' – which is the reflection of the glory of God – 'over one sinner that repenteth' (*Luke 15:10*). Each sinner who is saved becomes a joint-heir with Jesus Christ. Although it may be beyond our understanding, individually we have immense significance for God.

But although we exist for Him and because of Him, it is also true that we exist for others. Our Lord made this quite as clear as the point concerning our personal significance for Him. He said to His disciples, 'You are the light of the world. A city set on a hill cannot be hid' (*Matt. 5:14*). Or again, He said, 'Nor do men light a candle and put it under a bushel, but on a stand, and it gives light to all in the house. Let your light so shine before men that they may see your good works and glorify your Father who is in heaven' (*verses 15-16*). 'You are the salt of the earth; but if the salt has lost its taste, how shall its saltness be restored? It is no longer good for anything except to be thrown out and trodden under foot by men' (*verse 13*). So it is quite clear in the Scriptures that not only have you and I significance as far as God is concerned, but that we have significance for others around us. Indeed, it seems to me that God is saying to us, His own children, that we are special people in this world. What has happened to us is so great and so wonderful that we are to be as a light in the world, a city that is set upon a hill which *cannot* be hid.

What an immense challenge this is to us all when we claim to be the kind of people that we say we are spiritually – the children of God, temples of the Holy Spirit. It brings home to us the fact that every Christian should be a 'man for others'. It is this truth which sprang to Paul's mind as he wrote from prison to the Philippian church. You remember that he had been reminding this church of the necessity to be united, to love one another, that their names were written in heaven; and this, in turn, seems to have caused him to urge them to rejoice in the greatness and gloriousness of what God had done for them – 'Rejoice in the Lord always; again I will say, Rejoice.' He went on from there to say that it is not only in our own hearts and minds that we should be rejoicing, but that those around us should see the effect of this relationship which we have with God lived out in our daily lives; that what has happened to us spiritually has so changed and affected us that those around us *must* see the outcome of it. The particular quality that Paul had in mind here is called forbearance. He said to the Philippians, 'Let *all* men know your forbearance' or 'Let your forbearance be known unto all men'. There is something fundamental about this which springs from a common source, and so I will deal here with the meaning of the word 'forbearance', the example of forbearance, and the source of forbearance.

THE MEANING OF FORBEARANCE

In the first place it was Paul's assumption that this forbearance was theirs to make known to others. It was part of them, that is, it was the way in which they were in Christ. It was not something which was artificially put on but *an essential part of their Christian character*. Before we go any further let us note that Paul said, 'Let *your* forbearance be known to all men'. This is not somebody else's forbearance that we are to admire, but it is a quality which Paul considered *every Christian* in Philippi should possess. He did not say there were some of them who had got the gift of forbearance, there were some of them who had got this kind of temperament. He was speaking to *every* Christian in the Philippian church and the same word speaks to us today: 'Let *your* forbearance be known to all men.'

It is a Greek word that is very rarely used in the Scriptures and there is not a translation for it in the English language. This is so in many languages. I think of the Welsh word 'hwyl' which we talk about in preaching and there is no single word in English to convey what we mean by it in Welsh. In the same way, there is something here that the English language cannot convey in one word, although there was a Greek word for it. It was an expression for a man's balanced, intelligent and decent outlook in contrast to that of the licentious man. It was also used for a considerate, thoughtful attitude in legal matters, that which is prepared to mitigate the rigours of the law – to temper justice with mercy. It expressed the attitude which is the opposite of demanding one's rights, the opposite of the attitude of Shylock in *The Merchant of Venice*, where Shakespeare in his inimitable way brings out the grasping, rigorous attitude of mind which Shylock had when he wanted his pound of flesh according to the law. You remember Portia's speech: 'The quality of mercy is not strained,/ It droppeth as the gentle rain from heaven.' So this word calls to mind noble-mindedness, meekness in the face of insults, mercifulness in judgment as opposed to harshness, anger, brutality and self-assertion. On the other occasion when this word is used, Paul talks of the gentleness of Christ. He was saying to this church that there ought to be a nobility, a balanced behaviour, an absence of this grasping or asserting of one's rights. This gentleness should be a characteristic which everybody can see in a Christian. So, of course, we all ought to be examining ourselves.

I must confess that when I was preparing this sermon during the week I looked back on my life and I could see ways and times when I had not been as gentle as I ought to have been. I may have been right in principle in what I was thinking and right in what I was doing, but I was wrong in my attitude. I think all of us need to come and face the word of God, let it speak to us and convict us, ask ourselves whether this forbearance is part of us and if not, why not? Because if it is not present, I believe there is something fundamentally wrong with us spiritually. Perhaps our faith is not genuine, and deep down we do not believe that what has happened to us in Christ is really true. Are we quenching the Spirit or hiding our light under a bushel? Do we give in to the fear of what others will think and so neglect our opportunities, or do we let sin rule and our old nature be uppermost? It may be that we are intelligent schizophrenics, that we are in a situation where, from the point of view of intelligence, we feel that our lives cannot be influenced by what we believe as Christians, and this is fatal.

In the Old Testament, when it was translated into the Greek Septuagint, the word that was used means 'gentle'. It was used to describe God's gentleness in dealing with us: 'The Lord, a God merciful and gracious, slow to anger, and abounding in steadfast love and faithfulness' (*Exod. 34:6*). 'For thou, Lord, art good and forgiving, abounding in steadfast love to all who call on thee' (*Ps. 86:5*). In 2 Corinthians 10:1 Paul wrote, 'I, Paul, myself entreat you, by the meekness and gentleness of Christ'. This is the word, the 'gentleness' of Christ. We read in Titus that the Christians were 'to speak evil of no one, to avoid quarrelling, to be gentle, and to show perfect courtesy toward all men' (*Tit. 3:2*). James in his epistle wrote, 'The wisdom from above is first pure, then peaceable, gentle' (*James 3:17*). The effect upon us of the wisdom of God should be that we become gentle. So the main impression that one has is of a sense of the gentleness of Christ. Where else can we find a better example of what Paul meant than by taking the very example that he himself took when he said, 'I Paul myself beseech you by the meekness and gentleness of Christ' (*2 Cor. 10:1*)? So it is to this example of the Lord Jesus that I turn your attention.

THE GENTLENESS OF CHRIST

Let us consider very briefly this tenderness and gentleness of the Lord Jesus Christ in His attitude towards people in various situations. There was no carping or self-righteous criticism in His attitude towards the woman taken in adultery. He did not defend her sin but He defended her because of the way in which she was being dealt with by the hypocritical Pharisees. So He said to her, 'Neither do I condemn thee: go, and sin no more' (*John 8:11*). When the woman who had been a sinner anointed Him with oil, there were those who criticized her and called her action a waste, but the Lord Jesus said, 'Let her alone; why do you trouble her? . . . She has done what she could; she has anointed my body beforehand for burying' (*Mark 14:6–8*). He dealt with the incident very gently both as regards those who were criticizing and indeed with the woman herself. Then there was Zacchaeus who was, after all, a twister, a robber and a thief, who had been robbing people of their money by his extortionate tax collecting; but there was a change in him. He wanted to see Jesus, and when He passed by He said, 'Zacchaeus . . . come down; for I must stay at your house today' (*Luke 19:5*). There was not one word of condemnation, but the very presence of the Lord Jesus transformed him and he said, 'Behold, Lord, the half of my goods I give to the poor; and if I have defrauded anyone of anything, I restore it fourfold' (*verse 8*). How gently the Lord Jesus dealt with these people. Because He had a sensitivity to all those who suffered, their anguish affected Him. He knew that He was going to raise Lazarus from the dead and yet when Mary and Martha came to Him He was touched by their suffering and even wept Himself. Again when the widow of Nain lost her only son, He was moved with compassion and said, '"Do not weep." And he came and touched the bier . . . And he said, "Young man, I say to you, arise." And the dead man sat up, and began to speak' (*Luke 7:13–15*). These are only a few examples of the gentleness and compassion of our Lord.

Moreover, the Lord Jesus dealt with the perplexities of His disciples with gentleness, and He understood the sense of desolation that was taking hold of them, their fear of losing Him, their need of comfort. They could not understand the providences of God which at that time meant that He was going to be taken from them, but He told them that He was not going to leave them orphans: 'Let not your hearts be troubled; you believe in God, believe also in me . . . I will not leave you desolate; I will come to you' (*John 14:1, 18*). When He washed their feet and Peter could not understand what He was doing and said, 'Lord, do you wash my feet?', Jesus said, 'What I am doing you do not know now, but afterward you will understand' (*John 13:6–7*). How gentle the Lord Jesus was in dealing with Peter. Even when He was surrounded by crowds and people were calling after Him and wanting miracles to be performed, He found time to be patient and tender with the little children. Sometimes we are so impatient as though all wisdom, power, knowledge and understanding, both spiritual and otherwise, had been given to us. We become impatient with people, we suffer fools far from gladly and, of course, behind this attitude there is a great root of pride – a sense of being superior to others. The word in the Greek conveys the gentleness of Jesus, His courtesy. You do not find one instance where the Lord Jesus Christ barges into another person's life. He never imposed Himself or His views in a harsh, belligerent way. He said, 'Behold, I stand at the door, and knock: if any man hear my voice, and open the door, I will come in to him and will sup with him' (*Rev. 3:20*). He told the fig tree to wither and bear no fruit, but He never said that to any human being, never.

Again, He was thoughtful about other people's needs. When He had preached to the 5,000 people, His disciples wanted Him to send them away into the villages around to buy their own food. But he realized their immediate need for food and He fed them Himself with the five loaves and the two fishes. The supreme example of His thoughtfulness was when He was hanging upon the cross with all the pain and suffering, of which we can barely guess; He was still able to say to John, 'Look after my mother'; and to His mother, 'Woman behold thy son.' His attitude to people in need was always one of courtesy, tenderness, and gentleness.

The Philippians were living in a society which, in some ways, was tougher and cruder than ours, but Paul told them to let *all* men see their forbearance – not only the Christians. In society today there is a very definite attitude of standing up for one's rights. There is the idea that we have a *right* to expect the State to do everything for us. Even in the life of the church people feel they have a *right* to be noticed, appreciated, and consulted. If you look at the life of the Lord Jesus I remind you that He waived His right to be the Lord of glory –

'Christ Jesus, who, though he was in the form of God, did not count equality with God a thing to be grasped, but emptied himself, taking the form of a servant, being born in the likeness of men. And being found in human form he humbled himself and became obedient unto death, even death on a cross' (*Phil. 2:5–8*). We believe all this and yet we push for what we consider to be our rights. When the Lord Jesus was being manhandled, completely against the rights of common justice since He was innocent, what happened when they came to take Him? He said, 'Do you think that I cannot appeal to my Father, and he will at once send me more than twelve legions of angels?' (*Matt. 26:53*). Why did He not do it? Because He waived His rights; He had come to die. There are times when, for spiritual reasons, we must waive our rights. There are more important issues than these rights that we stand up for; there are spiritual issues which may have to come before them. Mercy and justice must go together and, of course, in this context you can see that our Lord refused to be delivered.

Do not think that there is not a great relevance in what I am saying. I find there are some Christians today who are talking in terms of revolution, violent revolution, and they believe that the Christian church must be involved in this revolution. But I cannot find support for this idea in the Word of God. The Lord Jesus accomplished His purposes by His gentleness and sacrificial life. He fulfilled the prophecy of Isaiah who said, 'He will not wrangle or cry aloud, nor will any one hear his voice in the streets; he will not break a bruised reed or quench a smouldering wick' (*Matt. 12:19–20; Isa. 42:2–3*). A bruised reed is so fragile, yet He would not break it; a smoking wick gives so little light, yet He would not put it out. As He went into Jerusalem He knew that, by right, He was king but He went in, meek and lowly, riding upon an ass. We forget that the Jews were a subjugated people; the Romans ruled the country; it did not belong to the Jewish people any longer. But I cannot find one word of the Lord Jesus where He said that He would incite His people to violent means in order to establish His kingdom.

These are some examples of the forbearance and gentleness of Jesus Christ to guide and convict us. Earlier I maintained that this forbearance and gentleness about which Paul was talking ought to be part of us too. The gentleness of the Lord Jesus was not weakness; there were times when He was strong enough. He put out those who sold goods in the temple; He withstood all the opposition of the religious leaders to His ministry and He withstood them to the end even when they crucified Him. It is not weakness about which I am talking; it is something which has happened to us, something we have experienced, something which has changed us.

THE SOURCE OF FORBEARANCE

You may ask how this change takes place in us, and so I come to what I may call the source of gentleness. It comes to us in the first place *from the very nature of God Himself*. This is how God has displayed Himself in His treatment of us; He has restrained His anger towards us despite our sin and rebellion against Him, and He has dealt with us in accordance with His own nature. Despite our rejection of Him I see His patience with us, His longsuffering. If He exerted His rights He could have destroyed us, but He has chosen to save us. 'What if God, desiring to show his wrath and to make known his power, has endured with much patience the vessels of wrath made for destruction, in order to make known the riches of his glory for the vessels of mercy, which he has prepared beforehand for glory, even us whom he has called, not from the Jews only but also from the Gentiles?' (*Rom. 9:22–24*).

Moreover, He has shown us what the coming of the Lord Jesus means for us. In other words, He has shown us *the potential of humanity*. Not only in the life of the Lord Jesus, but in His resurrection, He has opened our eyes to see something of what, as human beings, we are going to be, and it is marvellous. 'I consider that the sufferings of this present time are not worth comparing with the glory that is to be revealed to us' (*Rom. 8:18*). So, if every time you look at another human being you remember what God has purposed for them, what indeed they *could* be by the grace of God, are you going to be aggressive towards them for the sake of an opinion? The gentleness of Christ is based upon what we are as human beings, created in the image of God. Let us look around us and see that person who is next door to us and who annoys us, and ask ourselves whether we help them or hinder them. Do we convey to them something of what we believe we are as human beings, created by God in His image and for His glory? When we look at those around us, let us remember what we were and what we would be but for the grace of God. You remember the parable of the unforgiving servant who was forgiven the £10 million, and the servant who owed him about £10 or some comparatively small sum of money. The lord forgave the one who owed millions but he, in turn, could not forgive the one who owed him £10! He did not take his own forgiveness seriously and the Lord Jesus condemned him. It is the same with you and me, this gentleness, this forbearance is not something we put on artificially; *it stems from the way we have been treated by God*, from what He has shown us, what He has done for us.

It seems to me that it is not an accident that Paul says in the next little phrase, 'The Lord is at hand.' Above and beyond all this there is the assurance that *God knows what my destiny is*. My life is not in the hands of human beings; my life is in the hands of God. People may think they can do this or that to me, but in the end nothing can come to me except through the hands of God, and my eyes are on those hands. 'Vengeance is mine,' says the Lord, 'I will repay.' Let us leave it to Him and when the Lord is at hand He will deal with those who need it and I can leave the matter to Him as Jesus Christ did with those who crucified Him.

This forbearance and gentleness of spirit is *consistent with a life lived in the light of the second coming*, knowing that in the day of judgment we will be answerable to God for our actions, knowing that to be a Christian means that Christ's life is in us. Paul is setting before us the gentleness of Christ and if, indeed, this is to be a continuing quality in us, among one another and to those around us, you can see we need to be very close to the same Lord Jesus. We need His life to be in us, we need His Spirit to possess us more and more, we need to know Him day by day in His gentleness. May God help us to see that Paul is setting before us forbearance and gentleness so that all men should see God in us. My dear brothers and sisters in Christ, let us live as the children of God.

6

The Impossible Imperative

Have no anxiety about anything, but in everything by prayer and supplication with thanksgiving let your requests be made known to God. Philippians 4:6

Have no anxiety about anything! Is this an impossible imperative? Paul has been setting before the Philippian church truths which could change not only them, but the world, from being a battleground into a foretaste of heaven. In the first verses of this chapter he urged them to be united in the Lord (*verses 2–3*), then to rejoice in the Lord always (*verse 4*), and to show the gentleness of Christ (*verse 5*). Now he puts before them freedom from anxiety, almost as a command. Was this an *impossible* imperative? Was it an *impossible* command? Is it realistic to 'be careful for nothing'?

THE IMPOSSIBLE IMPERATIVE

First of all, I want to be clear about what this command does *not* mean. It does not mean that we are not to care about our responsibilities – either natural or spiritual ones. We *are* meant to be concerned about these practical everyday things in our lives – families, work, friends, churches and so on – in the same way as Paul writes to these Philippians about the care he has for them. It does not mean the avoidance of any natural responsibilities; this is something quite different. The word translated by 'anxiety' does not really mean careful but full of care, that is gnawing worry, feverish anxiety, 'harassing care' (Lightfoot) – something which disturbs our peace, destroys our joy and makes us so burdened that we are sick with worry.

First of all, let us consider two important points about anxiety. First, anxiety is a natural reaction, and we would not be human if, faced with certain situations, we were not anxious. It may be that a person is facing a serious operation, family or financial worries, redundancy and unemployment, opposition, persecution, or even death; it may be that there is an important decision to be made about the future and we cannot yet see which is the right way to take. Of course we are anxious; we are only human. Secondly, it is foolish for us to say to people in such a situation, 'Cheer up, stop worrying'. The facts of the situation usually warrant anxiety and, anyway, we can never dictate to another person's feelings. People cannot 'snap-out' of their anxiety any more than a person with a broken leg can get up and walk.

So is there an answer to anxiety? The text here says, 'Have no anxiety about anything', but – and here is one of Paul's great 'buts' – he tells these Philippians that instead of remaining in a state of anxiety, 'in everything, by prayer and supplication with thanksgiving let your requests be made known unto God'. So he is saying to them, 'I am setting before you *an alternative to anxiety*'. In one statement: *the answer to care is prayer*. The cure for worry is prayerful worship; that is the way to deal with something which is very practical and which faces us all every day. Let us remember that this letter to the Philippians was not written from some Roman palace by a man who was surrounded by luxury and servants. It was written when Paul was in prison, where he was chained, where he had been deprived of all human and spiritual fellowship, when he could have been facing an immediate execution sentence. Yet he is the one who is saying, 'Have no anxiety about anything', but 'by prayer and supplication let your requests be made known unto God'. This was his testimony in the situation – *prayer has changed my anxiety into peace*.

THE PRACTICE OF PRAYER

So we need to examine very carefully this whole question of prayer. Many of us have probably prayed about things and it does not seem to have made any difference; God did not change the circumstances. We have all heard other people say the same thing – prayer did not change their circumstances. Where have we gone wrong?

Let us remember three things:

1. The circumstances with Paul did not change. He was still in prison; he was still chained to Roman soldiers; he was still uncertain as to whether or not he would be executed; and his circumstances were the result of a life-time of serving the Lord Jesus Christ! *The circumstances did not change, but Paul changed*.

2. Moreover, the experience of Paul is reinforced by the lives of people in the church; martyrs died praising God, glorifying Him in death. There have been hymn-writers such as William Cowper who wrote as his testimony:

> *Prayer makes the darkened cloud withdraw,*
> *Prayer climbs the ladder Jacob saw,*
> *Gives exercise to faith and love,*
> *Brings every blessing from above.*

To move nearer to the present, let us remember Hudson Taylor, the founder of the China Inland Mission (now the Overseas Missionary Fellowship). What responsibilities must have been upon him in his task of reaching the millions in China with the gospel! Not only did he have peace himself but he was able to help other people find it. George Müller ran a large orphanage in Bristol without any visible means of support and, in addition, helped to support many missionaries overseas. Providing the daily needs of all the children and staff at the orphanage could have been enough to drive him to distraction. But he was a man who lived a life of great peacefulness in the presence of his God without being overburdened with anxiety. How did these men find this peace? The answer is that they were great men of prayer.

3. In addition, we have as our greatest pattern the Lord Jesus Christ Himself who, when He was faced with the cross and all that it was going to mean to Him, went into the garden of Gethsemane to meet with His Father in prayer, and He came out of it with peace of mind and heart. With that peace He faced the rejection of people, the trial, the travesty of justice, the mocking, the scourging, the crown of thorns, and even the cross itself. He knew all these things would come and yet there was a peace about Him as He went to the cross. The circumstances did not change but in the garden, in prayer with His Father, He came to terms with the cares which would come upon Him.

We can see from the experience of the Lord Jesus Christ, the apostle Paul and others, that we need to look very closely at the meaning and use of prayer. Bearing this in mind, I believe there are a number of lessons to be learned from this text.

'IN EVERYTHING'

It says, 'Have no anxiety about anything but *in everything* . . .' A Christian should pray about everything. The Bible says, 'Cast *all* your anxieties on him' (1 Pet. 5:7). If anything is big enough to be a worry to you, whether it is large or small in the eyes of other people, it is big enough for you to take it back to God in prayer. The devil has been very subtle in this respect; he suggests to us that God does not care about the details of our lives – He is a *great* God. How can we bring our petty troubles into His presence? Are we carnal and immature Christians if we bring such trifles to God in prayer? There are several answers to this question.

1. Life is made up of little things, trials or tribulations of all sorts *and* sizes, and to cut God out of them is to cut God out of the greater part of our lives, which is what many of us are doing. Paul says 'in everything'. Life consists far more of the many little things than it does of the occasional big things.

2. Many small worries added together can be overwhelming, so each one of them has significance, and if only one of them is sufficient to disrupt our peace and fellowship with God then it is important enough for us to be concerned about it.

3. God states explicitly that He *is* concerned with small things. It was the Lord Jesus who said that not a sparrow falls to the ground without His Father knowing; that the very hairs of our head are all numbered. He told us to pray for our 'daily bread'. He *is* concerned about all these small things because they are vital to us, they are part of our lives. He saw the sorrow in the heart of the widow of Nain as she watched her only son taken for burial, and He was moved with compassion. Even on the cross there came into His heart a concern for His mother, that she would be lonely, and He told John to look after her. Is God concerned with little things like loneliness? This was the Son of God. To say that God is not interested in little things is to reject God's word and example. To think that He is not interested in the details of our lives is false spirituality. He said, 'I do *nothing* without my Father.' Do not let us try to be more spiritual than the Lord Jesus Christ. Paul says that God *knows* about the details of your lives – go back to Him about them.

4. Whether they are big or small worries which are left in our lives, unrelated to God, they all take on big proportions. The mistake of Saul and the whole army of Israel, including all

his great men, was that they measured Goliath with themselves, but David measured Goliath with God. 'Who is this uncircumcised Philistine that he should defy the armies of the living God?' (*1 Sam. 17:26*). No wonder the devil does not want us to bring our problems, great or small, to God, because he does not want us to see them in their proper perspective. But that is the way to see them as they affect the children of God. David immediately brought *God* into the situation and this altered everything. When he went forward he went with *God* in his mind.

5. Prayer is the way to turn our anxieties into the means of grace. The very worries themselves carry us back to God; they become the words of our prayers. Paul says that every anxiety is a personal invitation from God to come before Him in prayer, to call us back into His presence, to talk to Him about it.

DETAILED ADVICE ON PRAYER

Obviously the function of the kind of prayer that Paul had in mind was dynamic and he uses four different words to describe it.

Prayer is the general word used for offering up our desires and wishes to God, but it has one very vital mark – it is always God-centred. It is never used except as an address towards God. Too many of our prayers are godless! It is not that they are not directed towards God but that God is not in the forefront of our minds as He ought to be when we pray. We do not obey the pattern of our Lord's prayer – 'Our Father who art in heaven, hallowed be thy name'. He taught us that the first act is to meditate on the One to whom we are praying before we rush in with our requests. Notice how the Collects bring the person of God before us first of all: 'Almighty and everlasting God, who dost govern all things in heaven and earth; mercifully hear the supplications of thy people'.

'Almighty God, who through thy only-begotten Son Jesus Christ hast overcome death, and opened unto us the gate of everlasting life; we humbly beseech thee . . .' That is the way to pray. Perhaps we do not allow ourselves enough time in prayer in order to bring God into the situation at the very beginning. Another vital point in connection with this is that we should read our Bibles regularly and systematically, and meditate on them, because it is in this way that we come to know and understand the character of God, and it is this knowledge of God that we call to mind as we begin to pray.

The second word that Paul uses is *supplication*. It has more than the meaning of just making a request or petition to God; there is an overtone – a sense of need and human inadequacy, an urgent need which God alone can supply, so there is also a sense of humility before Him – we cannot command God but simply beseech Him. Supplication involves the whole personality of man, his mind, heart and will. Our prayers must come not only from our lips but from the depths of our beings, realizing that as children of God we have a right to come into His presence and bring our petitions before Him.

The third word is *requests*. If we are bowed down with cares and anxieties surely, when we come into God's presence, it is natural that we should tell Him *all* that we are concerned about, our detailed and definite requests. On Mount Carmel Elijah tells God exactly what he wants: 'Send the fire.' When Elisha was surrounded by the kings of Syria and he was in a desperate position, he said, 'Lord, open their eyes.' God has extended to us the privilege of bringing *every* need before Him in prayer: 'Let your requests be made known unto God' – not just *some* of your requests!

Finally, we pray *with thanksgiving*. That little phrase of two words is the most searching examination of our attitude to God. Let us remember the prison, the chains, the food, the possible death sentence – how could Paul say, 'Thank you, Lord'? Are we to say 'Thank you, Lord' in the midst of anxieties and trouble? The answer is yes. We can thank Him for the past mercies and present mercies, and to them we can add, as undoubtedly the apostle did, the eternal mercies, the *unchangeable mercies of God*. Paul knew that he was forgiven, he was restored, he was the heir of everlasting life, that there was a crown of glory waiting for him whatever happened in his earthly life. He also thanked God for the present mercies because he knew that 'all things work together for good to them that love God, to them who are the called according to his purpose' (*Rom. 8:28*). He had written those words himself from God. We may be worried about our present condition but we can thank God because He has assured us that it *is* working for our good and His word *is* truth. We can pray, 'Lord, take it from me or give me the grace to bear it; supply whatever strength I need to go through this test and the grace that I need to use it to Thy glory.' Thankfulness takes the bitterness against God out of our hearts. It overrides the temptation to think that God does not care. It is the test of a loving son going back to a loving Father with faith in Him who rules and controls *everything*, and saying, 'I may not understand what is happening but I know You care. Somehow or other You have a purpose for me in all this.' Thankfulness gives us a positive attitude of mind; prayer with thanksgiving is an expression of our faith in the goodness of the God who sent His Son to die upon the cross for us.

The apostle told the Philippians: 'Be anxious for nothing . . . And the peace of God . . . *will* keep your hearts and your minds in Christ Jesus.' Here is an opportunity for us to find in our own experience that prayer *can* cure worry because it has brought God into the situation.

7
Peace – The Perfect Possession

Have no anxiety about anything, but in everything by prayer and supplication with thanksgiving let your requests be made known to God. And the peace of God, which passes all understanding, will keep your hearts and your minds in Christ Jesus.

Philippians 4:6–7

We have looked at verse 6, the impossible imperative, 'Have no anxiety about anything', but we are now going to consider the very positive aspect of this verse: peace – the perfect possession. Paul used this word a great deal in his ministry. Spurgeon wrote of him, 'He loved peace, preached peace, lived peace, died in peace, and behold he hath entered into the fruition of peace and dwells in peace before the throne of God.' Time and time again the apostle begins and ends his epistles with 'Grace to you and peace from God'. He uses it in many places, for example, 'Live in peace, and the God of love and peace shall be with you' (*2 Cor. 13:11*). Let us also remember that Paul was writing this letter to the Philippians from a Roman prison, facing possible execution, burdened with the cares of the church, guarded by Roman soldiers, with enough problems to take away the peace of any man and fill him with anxiety. Yet here he was telling these Philippians not only how to deal with anxieties but how their anxieties could be replaced by the peace of God. Some commentators think that this verse is linked with verses 1–6 and, in a way, I believe they are right, because these are spiritual conditions: that is, standing fast in the Lord, unity, rejoicing, gentleness of Christ, supplication with thanksgiving. These all contribute to a state of peace. However, it seems to me that the 'and' at the beginning of verse 7 is part of verse 6, so it would run, 'Let your requests be made known to God *and* the peace of God which passes all understanding will keep your hearts and your minds in Christ Jesus.' In other words, there is the state of anxiety, but the antidote is prayer and through this means, which God has made possible to us, He is able to impart *His own peace* to us. Let us briefly recall what has been said previously. Paul said that the answer to anxieties is that we should bring everything to God in prayer, *everything*. Secondly, our prayers should be God-centred prayers, and thirdly, they should be prayers of supplication, whole-hearted prayers. So often our prayers are made only with our lips and not with our hearts as well. Fourthly, they should be requests – detailed prayers; and finally, our prayers should be based on a thankfulness of spirit for God's past mercies, present mercies and the promise of mercies to come. I believe it is when we come to grips with prayer in this way that God, for His part, will give us His peace 'which passes all understanding'.

THE PEACE OF GOD

In the first place, let us be clear what this does not mean. *It does not mean peace with God.* Paul is not at this point concerned with a man's relationship with God; he is concerned with something subjective, experiential, a condition of the heart, a consciousness of peace whose source is God. Peace is something which all of us want. In fact, the majority of mankind is seeking peace in one way or another and each one of us in different ways wants peace. So let us try to understand what Paul is telling these Philippians who, after all, lived in a situation which in some ways was similar to our own. They were in a heathen environment, under pressure; there were all sorts of false religions around them, all kinds of temptations; it was a decadent society with a great deal of corruption. These Philippians were not living in some ideal situation, they were human beings like ourselves, and yet Paul is talking to them about the peace of God which overcomes all anxieties. What does he mean by these words, 'the peace of God'?

Peace comes to man only as God's gift, and one of the great characteristics of the kingdom of God, the Messianic kingdom, is that it is to be a kingdom of peace (*Isa. 11:1–9*), and the Lord Jesus is called 'the Prince of Peace'. 'For to us a child is born, to us a son is given . . . and his name will be called . . . Prince of Peace' (*Isa. 9:6*). So we find this thought of the peace of God running through the whole Bible, especially in the Psalms: 'Let me hear what God the Lord will speak, for he will speak peace to his people . . . Steadfast love and faithfulness will meet; righteousness and peace will kiss each other' (*Psa. 85:8, 10*). Here are a few examples of Paul's writing: 'The God of peace be with you all' (*Rom. 15:33*); 'The God of peace shall bruise Satan under your feet shortly' (*Rom. 16:20*); 'For God is not the author of confusion, but of peace' (*1 Cor. 14:33*); 'Now may the God of peace who brought again from the dead our Lord Jesus, the great shepherd of the sheep . . .' (*Heb. 13:20*). In other words, as much as God is thought of as the God of love and mercy, the God of holiness, so we are to think of Him as the God of peace. What does this word 'peace' mean in Scripture?

The classical Greek word had a rather negative meaning, that is peace as the antithesis of war. But used in the Hebrew sense – 'shalom' – it was very positive. It was the greeting used by one Jew to another, and the basic meaning is wholeness, the well-being that comes from God, including all the blessings of God given in life – peaceful conditions, tranquillity, prosperity, salvation. All these meanings are included in this word 'shalom' – peace. As a greeting it meant, 'May all the blessings of God be upon you, so that there may be a wholeness about your life which is glorifying to God' – that is, that we may enjoy the fullness of blessings, and as Christians, we are what God intends us to be as His redeemed ones.

Let us think about these words 'the peace *of God*'. As I have already said, 'the peace of God' and 'peace with God' are two different things altogether. The words 'peace with God' assume that we have been reconciled to God and we know that peace with God which has come about through Christ. Romans 5:1 tells us that 'since we are justified by faith, we have peace with God through our Lord Jesus Christ'. The enmity between God and man, caused by our own sinfulness, has been dealt with, taken away by the sacrificial death of Christ on our behalf. He was our substitute on the cross and we know that we are reconciled to God because His righteousness is the ground of our acceptance before God. 'God was in Christ reconciling the world to himself' (*2 Cor. 5:19*). We are 'accepted in the beloved' (*Eph. 1:6*). We are at peace with God; our status is that of being His children.

But *the peace of God* is different. We are not talking about our standing before God but about our present condition, something which God has given us *of Himself*. It seems to me that God is seeking to give us part of His very character and being. He is a God of peace and He imparts that peace to us. When God says, 'Be ye holy: for I am holy' (*1 Pet. 1:16*), He wants us to have the same nature as Himself, to be 'partakers of the divine nature' (*2 Pet. 1:4*), which is created in righteousness. In the same way the Lord Jesus said, 'Peace I leave with you; my peace I give to you; not as the world gives do I give to you' (*John 14:27*). He wants to give us the very state of heart and mind that He had; He promised it! Something which is characteristic of the Lord Jesus, which has its source in God, is to become ours – the *peace of God*.

The infinite nature of God is infinite repose. God *is* what we are always striving to attain – peace and rest – but God is at perfect rest within Himself. He said '*I am*', not 'I am becoming'. There is no fret, no feverishness in the activities of God, there is no striving for unobtainable goals, no discord between His love and justice, no conflict between His mercy and power. God is a God of peace. In other words, there is an inner harmony in God, there is a perfect integration between all His attributes; there is perfect tranquillity. He is perfect in wholeness, in love, in joy and in peace. But God wants *us* to have this peace, which is His peace, in our hearts and minds. An analogy is impossible but we know that in a well-oiled machine there is great activity but no jarring; everything functions in the way in which it was intended. God is at perfect rest within Himself. There is no conflict between one part of His character and another. There is no striving between His goals and His ability to perform them.

In contrast to God, man allows his anxieties to get out of perspective and dominate his mind; he loses his peace and joy and even his usefulness in service, which is the opposite of God's peace. But here we see Paul in tranquillity, putting his life in the hands of God, knowing what could come upon him and yet he had the peace of God, an assurance that God's purposes would be fulfilled, that his life was in God's hands, all the circumstances were in God's hands, and he had the peace of God; it had taken possession of him.

The Lord Jesus, on the night before He was crucified, knew that His disciples would fail and betray Him. He knew that He was going to endure a mockery of trials, to be crowned with thorns, mocked and laughed at, nailed to a cross, and surrounded by jeering crowds, and yet He said, 'My peace I leave with you.' God's purpose was going to be fulfilled, His Father's love possessed His heart. He had complete trust in what His Father had purposed, He *knew* He was going in the way His Father had destined, and He was absolutely at peace – He had the peace of God. Paul was talking in this verse about the peace of God, this perfect wholeness, this complete integration of God's peace with us; there is no conflict, it has all gone. For Christians there is to be a consciousness of being in the place where we should be, of being the kind of people God intends us to be, that we should have something of God's own perfection.

'PASSES ALL UNDERSTANDING'

Paul said that this peace of God which He has granted to us, passes all understanding. 'The peace of God transcends every human thought, surpassing all our dreams' (Moffatt). It is beyond comprehension but it is not irrational, because we know the grounds of it; it is deeper, broader, sweeter and more heavenly than human tongue can tell. Moreover it is a direct, immediate work of the Holy Spirit in the heart of man, a fruit of the Spirit, a gift of God. When we use the means of grace, especially prayer, it is as though God Himself is present in some inexplicable manner in the human heart, taking away all the anxieties. We possess not just consolation but the God of consolation, not merely peace but the God of peace. There is a consciousness of the presence of God bringing His own peace into our lives. When the old Scottish preacher Horatius Bonar was on his sick bed in great suffering, he knew the very presence of God with him, overcoming his anxieties, his pain and his weariness. He had no respite from pain but he experienced the peace of God which passes all understanding and he wrote the following verses:

Long days and nights upon this restless bed
Of daily, nightly weariness and pain,
Yet Thou art here, my ever-gracious Lord,
Thy well-known voice speaks not to me in vain:
'In me ye shall have peace'.

The darkness seemeth long, and even the light
No respite brings with it, no soothing rest
For this worn frame, yet in the midst of all
Thy love revives. Father, thy will is best.
'In me ye shall have peace'.

THE GARRISONED HEART

When Paul said this peace will keep our hearts and minds in a way beyond all that we can imagine, expect or reason out, he was thinking of the whole personality, because our thoughts and emotions come from our personality. In other words, *God will keep our whole being, our hearts, minds and wills in this peace*. The word that He used for keep is 'garrison'. He was saying that this peace of God which passes all understanding will garrison our hearts in Jesus Christ. In other words, He will protect us, He will keep off the enemy who would attack us. In all tribulations His peace will keep out the temptation to doubt and despair; it will protect us from the subtleties of the world as they come upon us. His peace will keep our minds centred on Jesus Christ, the Prince of peace, the One who said, 'My peace I am giving unto you'. It is the Lord Jesus who is our peace and our Redeemer. God loved us so much that He gave His only begotten Son to be associated with, and to take away, the sin of the world. He is the bread of life, the author of eternal life. He is the good Shepherd who cares for His sheep and lays down His life for them, and He is going to unite us with Himself so that we share eternity with Him. It is the peace of God in Jesus Christ which will garrison our hearts against the anxieties and temptations of the world.

When we say the benediction, 'The peace of God . . .', do we see the greatness, the wonder and the glory of what God has offered us in Jesus Christ, that His peace will keep our hearts and minds in that tranquillity, that wholeness, that glory which is of God? May God write these things upon our hearts. And let us spend more time with Him, praying as He taught us to pray. May each one of us know the truths of the Word that 'The peace of God which passes all understanding shall garrison our hearts and minds in Jesus Christ'. Let us listen to the voice of God and not the voice of the world, the flesh, and the devil.

8
Think About These Things

Finally, brethren, whatever is true, whatever is honourable, whatever is just, whatever is pure, whatever is lovely, whatever is gracious, if there is any excellence, if there is anything worthy of praise, think about these things. Philippians 4:8

No doubt you are aware that the apostle Paul has been presenting us, in this epistle, with some startling imperatives. In this chapter that we have been considering, you will remember that he started by telling us that we should 'stand firm in the Lord', 'agree in the Lord', and then that magnificent call to 'rejoice in the Lord always', and to 'have no anxiety about anything'. Now he brings another one before us. He says, 'Think about these things' – dwell in thought on them – and it is a present imperative. I can imagine the apostle Paul sitting in a Roman prison and, having pointed out the way of peace to these Philippians, he ends his letter with a variety of exhortations and thoughts. As he sees these people in his mind's eye, surrounded by a hostile, seducing world, he longs for them to remain in the peace of God. But he knows that this is not something automatic, that the peace of God has to be nurtured, in other words, *you have to walk in the ways of God if you want to continue in the peace of God*. But Paul knew, as I hope all of you will know before the end of this sermon, that walking with God is vitally connected with our thought-life. What do we think about? What are the thoughts we cultivate and allow? I want to highlight the importance of our thought-life as Christians.

Now it may well be that somebody will immediately say, 'I am a practical sort of person, down to earth, ordinary; I am not an intellectual. Do not come to me with a great deal of theoretical matter concerning thinking.' Well, this sermon *is* for you, because it is about something which is intensely practical, something which affects each and every one of us. The apostle Paul is telling us to '*think* about these things'. In these days the lives of so many people are intensely pressurized, changes are taking place so quickly; many are burdened with work, bowed down with trouble and care of one kind or another, either in careers or in their home lives, with very little time to reflect upon their thought-life. But I am still asking you to pause with me and consider the importance of our thought-life. I am concerned with what it is that occupies our minds more than anything else. What is it that our minds are active on, what is the subject-matter of our thinking throughout the day? *Much of our peace and much of our spirituality depends upon this.*

THE IMPORTANCE OF OUR THOUGHTS

1. In order that this should come home to us, let me first of all remind you that *God takes heed to our thoughts*. 'The thoughts of the wicked are an abomination to the Lord' (*Prov. 15:26*). It is not necessarily the deeds only but the *thoughts* of the wicked that are an abomination unto the Lord; He hates them. Moreover, our imagination is all part of our thinking. We read in Genesis, 'The Lord saw that the wickedness of man was great in the earth, and that every imagination of the thoughts of his heart was only evil continually' (*Gen. 6:5*). Let me give you some more quota-

tions from Scripture: 'The Lord knows the thoughts of man' (*Ps. 94:11*); 'For I know their works and their thoughts' (*Isa. 66:18*); 'Thou understandest my thought afar off' (*Ps. 139:2*). In Genesis 18:12–13 we read how God knew the thoughts of Sarah: 'So Sarah laughed *to herself*, saying, "After I have grown old, and my husband is old, shall I have pleasure?" The Lord said to Abraham, "Why did Sarah laugh, and say, 'Shall I indeed bear a child, now that I am old?'"' So although you may not think that God *is* concerned about your thoughts, the Bible tells us quite clearly that He *is* going to judge people, not only on account of their words and deeds but also their thoughts.

2. *The gospel is intimately concerned with our thoughts*. Part of the great work of the gospel is to bring every thought captive to Christ – 'to destroy strongholds. To destroy arguments and every proud obstacle to the knowledge of God, and take every thought captive to obey Christ' (*2 Cor. 10:4–5*). So if the gospel which you have received is not concerned with your thoughts it is a false gospel, whatever experiences you have had. What is the call of the gospel? 'Let the unrighteous man forsake' what? 'His thoughts' (*Isa. 55:7*). What is repentance but a change of heart and mind, that is a change in our way of thinking? You remember that when the prodigal son came to himself he thought, 'I have been a fool and I am going back home, I am going to live under my father's jurisdiction' (*Luke 15:17–19*). His whole mental approach changed. In other words, what the gospel is telling us is what Paul is saying to the Philippians. God *is* concerned about our thoughts. Paul says in Romans, 'Be ye transformed by the renewal of your mind' (*Rom. 12:2*). Does that not refer to our thinking, our thought-life? As David says in Psalm 119:59: 'I thought on my ways, and turned my feet unto thy testimonies.' So we can see that thinking is an essential part of the process of conversion because it involves our minds as well as our hearts. Indeed, if there has not been

a change there, one has got to ask the question, 'Has there been a change at all?'

3. Let us remember, too, that *the power to think is one of God's greatest gifts to us*, and marks us off, I believe, from the rest of creation. Man is made in the likeness of God with the ability to reason and make responsible decisions and choices. So surely it matters how we use this great gift that God has given us, whether we employ our thoughts in the things of God and for the glory of God and the extension of His kingdom, or whether we use them only in order to satisfy ourselves or to dishonour God.

4. There is another reason why the whole question of our thought-life should be examined carefully. *Our thoughts express what we really are* – we are what we think! We can easily deceive other people by our actions, we can be hypocritical in word and deed, but not in thought. The Bible tells us that the thoughts of our hearts reveal what we are more than anything else: 'As he thinketh in his heart, so is he' (*Prov. 23:7*); 'Keep your heart with all vigilance; for from it flow the springs of life' (*Prov. 4:23*). We can appear to be very spiritual, as the Pharisees did; you could not impeach their standard of life. They spent time in prayer, wore special clothes, kept the law, fasted, gave tithes, and so on, but these were all outward things. The Lord Jesus said that it is from the inside that the trouble comes: 'Out of the heart of man comes evil thoughts continually.' What the Pharisees were – truly were – was mirrored by their thoughts, their motives. It is our thoughts that are the key to our personalities; they reflect our true selves, the selves which only God knows, and it is our thoughts which motivate and govern our actions.

5. *The grace of God in all spiritual matters is essentially linked to our thoughts*. This involves our knowledge of the truth, especially as it is revealed in the Bible. To delight in the law of God, to meditate upon it, must involve thinking: it is through our minds that the Holy Spirit leads us into all

truth. Our thoughts precede our actions, so it is our thought-life which constitutes the greater part of our service to God. 'A book of remembrance was written for them that feared the Lord', and what else did they do? They '*thought* upon his name' (*Mal. 3:16*). These were the people whom God marked out; they thought about God, His character, His attributes, His being; they believed and loved Him and loved one another. To desire God, seeking to please Him, praying to Him, seeking to win others to Him, these all concern our thoughts. As Richard Baxter wrote, 'These are the principal parts of his service which are exercised immediately by our thoughts.' Moreover, it is only 'the pure in heart [who] shall see God' (*Matt. 5:8*). So if we want to find God, the change must begin in our thought-life. 'A broken and a contrite heart, O God, thou wilt not despise' (*Ps. 51:17*).

On the other hand, the mark of the ungodly is their mental rejection of God – 'A rebellious people, who walk in a way that is not good, after their own thoughts' (*Isa. 65:2*); or, as the psalmist said, 'The fool says in his heart [that is, he thinks], "There is no God"' (*Ps. 14:1*). A person may be very intelligent and learned, but in the eyes of God he can be a fool because of his thoughts. Many deceive themselves, said Paul, by thinking themselves to be something, when they are nothing (*Gal. 6:3*).

THE CONTROL OF OUR THOUGHTS

Our thoughts are our most constant activity. We think all day and every moment of the day; our thoughts are our constant occupation. Even if we sit in a chair and outwardly do nothing, we have to consciously think, unless we are fast asleep! So we are actively thinking all day from the moment we awake until the moment when we go to sleep at night; the one thing we are doing all day is thinking. It is the activity of our minds and it is *we* who think. We are responsible for our thoughts just as we are responsible for our outward actions. When Paul was concerned with what these people were thinking, he was concerned with something which was essentially a very practical and a very important part of their lives, and the same truth applies to us also.

Behind this text it is clear that the apostle assumes that our thoughts are subject to our wills and that we *can* control the way in which we think, and particularly the subject matter about which we think. He implies that we *can* devote ourselves to thinking about what is true, noble, just and lovely, and so on. The first commandment is, 'You shall love the Lord your God with all your heart, and with all your soul, and with all your mind, and with all your strength' (*Mark 12:30*). But, you know, I find that people say to me, 'I cannot *help* thinking like that.' There are times when this can be true, and it can be so for several reasons. (1) There are psychological reasons. When people are mentally ill, suffering from diseases of the mind, they cannot control their thoughts. These are a special category of people who need expert medical attention and treatment. (2) There are other people who are in various states of depression when morbid thoughts take hold of them which are very difficult to move, and they also need expert pastoral and/or medical help. But these are generally the exceptional cases; for the vast majority of us there are ways and means of controlling our thoughts. Paul was not writing to people who were in some special psychological condition; he was concerned with the normal condition of the mind. (3) Emotion is a wonderful gift of God to us but there are right and wrong emotions. Our minds can be carried away by strong feelings, so we must try to avoid the situations where wrong thoughts overcome us – take care what we read, what we watch, what we listen to and the friends whose company we choose. The mind responds to stimuli – it can be nurtured, moved and led into various pathways by what we choose to put before it. The apostle's plea here is that we keep the right things before our minds, namely, whatever is of God.

The apostle is saying that the mind, in fact, can be taught to think in certain ways, that there are *habits of thought*, good as well as bad. It is part of the learning process that we learn to think instinctively about certain things – the way in which we ride a bicycle or drive a car. He is concerned here that we take care to develop habits of thinking about the right things, about God and the things of God. The mind is not a computer, an impressive machine with a set programme of thought with which it is impossible to interfere. *As Christians, our minds are intended to be our servants, not we the slaves of our minds*. What is the essential element of being born of God? It means that there is a supernatural work of God which has taken place within us whereby our personality is reorientated towards God and the things of God. The New Testament says that a new creation has taken place in the man who is born again, so that his whole being, including his mind, is directed towards God. The Christian now has a new power so that he can pursue a new pathway to God, and he can keep to that pathway. 'Hence I remind you to rekindle the gift of God that is within you through the laying on of my hands; for God did not give us a spirit of timidity but a spirit of power and love and self-control' (*2 Tim. 1:6–7*). When a man is born again he is born of the Spirit of God; the Spirit dwells within him, and dwells within him for the very purpose that he should become like the Lord Jesus Christ. If the Lord Jesus is our perfect example let us go back to Him and ask the question, 'How did He live?' 'Were His thoughts directed towards His Father?' He said, 'The Son can do nothing of his own accord' (*John 5:19*); 'The words that I say to you I do not speak on my own authority; but the Father who dwells in me does his works' (*John 14:10*). His thought-life was controlled by His Father. The Bible is very clear – 'Let this mind be in you, which was also in Christ Jesus' (*Phil. 2:5*).

Now I know I am setting up a high standard, but the

standard has always been a high one for Christians. It *is* very hard, but I do not think that the Bible ever said that the Christian life would be easy. In fact, it says exactly the opposite – 'If any man would come after me, let him deny himself and take up his cross and follow me' (*Matt. 16:24*). It *is* difficult to love your enemies, your persecutors, those people who slander and abuse you, to love your neighbour as yourself and the person whose personality clashes with your own. It *is* a fight, it *is* a battle, but that does not mean to say that it is impossible or that we are not meant to attempt it and to continue to attempt it.

People get into the habit of thinking wrongly; they start in an atmosphere of unbelief at the beginning of the day. One of the best things about reading the Bible and praying first thing in the morning is to remind ourselves that we are God's people, it is God's day, and the circumstances that we are going to meet are those which God Himself allows us to meet, because He says that 'All things work together for good to those who love God' (*Rom. 8:28*). I find that some people think that Christianity is concerned with singing hymns, perhaps going to church occasionally, or just being nice friends together and occasionally doing good deeds. There is nothing more embracing, all-embracing, than the Christian gospel. It must affect every part of our lives and, as you can see, it goes right to the very centre of our being, to our thoughts, our motives, our imaginations. As our Lord said, 'You have heard that it was said, "You shall not commit adultery." But I say to you that every one who looks at a woman lustfully has already committed adultery with her in his heart' (*Matt. 5:27–28*). What will govern our thoughts during this coming week? Will our minds be filled with anxieties, envy, evil or unworthy imaginations, unkind thoughts, criticism of others, self-pity, self-centred thoughts, or will they be filled with thoughts about God? Paul's plea here is to put the right things before our minds –

whatever is honest, just, pure, lovely, gracious, worthy of praise – things which are God-centred and which will affect our attitude and actions towards God and towards other people.

DIFFICULTIES AND OBJECTIONS

Paul knew the very difficult situation in which these people were living. He knew the spirit of the age in which they lived and he wanted the Philippians to be perfectly clear that part of the way in which they were to remain in the peace of God was to see that they did not fall into the pattern of the life around them. They were living in an age when open promiscuity was rife, divorce was commonplace, homosexuality was accepted as a way of life, violence was a spectacle people paid to see when gladiators killed each other publicly; infanticide was practised; and the inhumanity of man to man was part of the general life-style.

In the Roman Empire, as we still see in our society today, there was also the influence of humanism. Natural desires were to be satisfied, including sexual desires. All that mattered was man's desires; he had no other term of reference but himself. We find people in our society today who subscribe to the belief that all morals are subjective, life is to be entirely man-centred. What man thinks is right for him *is* right, and what is wrong is what *he* believes is wrong. Many people express a desire and a right to be liberated from the constriction imposed by a high moral code of behaviour. They feel they have a right openly to sleep with whom they will and as often as they like, either male or female, with total disregard for the sanctity of marriage. Drug-taking and alcohol have become a way of life in order to obliterate the difficulties and pressures of life. But standards of society change, as we know so well; they change according to trends of thought. It is true that society makes certain laws to guide and protect us, but what we do personally is our own business and nobody can condemn us. Sometimes, however, our behaviour has repercussions and only bitter experience teaches people the error and bankruptcy of their ways – unhappiness on a personal level, broken homes, insecurity, loss of *true* liberty, loss of health, and even loss of life. In contrast to this, the Christian has an objective standard which does not change with the varying standards of society. *His standard is God's standard*, which is unchangeable because God is unchangeable. He is the Creator, He is holy, and man is answerable to Him. He has revealed His standards in the Bible and, as Christians, we must live by them.

Another objection may come to people's minds, and it is this: How can I keep my mind on the things of God when I have to concentrate on my work all day? The answer is twofold – firstly you cannot! Secondly, you are not expected to do so! You may say, 'You tell us to think about God and fill our minds with these things and then you say that I cannot possibly do that!' But there is not really a contradiction of terms here, because if your mind is engaged, as it ought to be, on the tasks that you have in hand for your daily work, obviously at that particular time you cannot be thinking about God directly; He knows this and does not expect it to be otherwise. But you must be aware that the work to which God has called you is to be done to His glory whether it be as a housewife, student, lecturer, teacher, minister, factory or office worker, or any other occupation. It includes *whatever work* God has given you to do as a Christian. It is the work that *God* has given you and you must be quite clear about this from the beginning. So the framework of your thought-life is that you are where God wants you to be, and the work that you are doing is the work that He has given you to do. It is an error, and one of the unfortunate things which evangelicals have been teaching for some time, that the *only* work that is

God's work is direct evangelism, something to do with the church, with religion, something which is done publicly, and this is entirely wrong. When Adam was in the garden, God set him to till the soil – *that* was the work which God gave him – there was no evangelizing to do! *It was in tilling the soil that Adam pleased God*. We *are* meant to be evangelists, but that can be done within the scope of our own particular calling; it can be done in obscurity among individuals. It is the way and the spirit in which we do the work given to us that is important. This is why, at the beginning of each day, we need to remind ourselves that this is God's day, this is the work that He has given us to do, and we are going to do it for this reason. Therefore, the framework of our lives and daily circumstances is the knowledge that God has put us where we are in order to do His work in that particular place. In this way God is not far from our thoughts at any time; in committing our day to Him we remind ourselves of these truths and learn to see Him in all the circumstances of our lives. However, it is not only when we are busy that our minds can be too occupied with everyday things. Our minds can be wrongly occupied even when we are not busy, such as in retirement or when we are alone – especially if we live alone. Our thoughts can still be self-centred, full of worries and self-pity, occupied only with trivialities which affect us as individuals: our difficulties, our problems, our feelings, our loneliness and so on, when we should be positively concerned about God, His kingdom, His glory, His world, His work and the needs of others, not just our own.

THE CHRISTIAN LIFE IS ALL-EMBRACING

Christianity must embrace everything, it must be concerned with every department of our lives, including our thought-life; all our activities are to be governed by the gospel. Behind it there is the great truth that God is the Creator of the world;

He is the Creator of man, of the universe and everything in it. So creation is the handiwork of God. It expresses His very being, and we must look at this world as God's world. All the gifts of this world must be appreciated and used as God's gifts (and the environmentalists have a point here). It also means that all other gifts such as music, literature and art, and human life with all its relationships, must come under the purview of being the gifts of our Creator. Consequently we are answerable to Him for what we do with these, and whether we are using them according to the way that God wants us to use them. This includes our minds, with all their potentiality. One day we shall be answerable to God for what we have done with His creation, of which we are a part. It is sin that has marred and perverted God's gifts to us, but the gospel tells us that the Lord Jesus came to deliver us from sin and to enable us to live as the children of God. The more we become like Him the more we shall find that we are able to live in this world as His true children, relating everything, including our minds, to the work of the Lord Jesus Christ. Moreover, the gospel includes the promise of the power of the Holy Spirit who dwells in us and enables us to live in this world so that we do not face life in an attitude of defeat or despair, but in the light of the Holy Spirit bringing peace into our lives and into our minds, in order that we may live God-centred lives in every way, including our thoughts. I believe it is important for us to realize what we are up against because this is a complete contrast to what is happening all around us; it is the opposite of the attitude of the non-Christian world. Paul knew this and we must understand it too and beware of the attacks of the world, the flesh and the devil.

THE MATTER WHICH IS TO OCCUPY OUR MINDS

We have been considering the importance of our thought-life, its possibilities, problems and responsibilities. We have seen that there is to be no restriction of any area of thought because this is God's world, and we are free to apply our minds to all of it – science, art, music, and so on. But we must also consider the moral standards which should govern our minds and use our critical faculties in order to be selective; we must allow God to guide us in what we choose to think about. We have been considering what we should not be thinking about and the difficulties of controlling our minds, but what *are* the things which the apostle tells the Philippians (and us) to think about? What are the things which are to dominate our minds, our hearts, our lives? The apostle gives us a number of very positive ways in which we should be thinking.

Whatever is true. The word in the Greek means not only truthfulness but what is real and genuine as opposed to what is false – things of substance as opposed to things of shadow. It is the word you would use when you say that the things of this world pass away, but the realities are eternal. Also, amid the round of our daily lives, in a godless world, we are to seek to maintain the most vital of all things – *the truth about God*, about eternity, the cross, the resurrection, the sinfulness of man, judgment and man's relationship to Jesus Christ as revealed in Scripture. But the Christian must not only be truthful towards God, he must also be truthful towards other people; we are to be examples of truth before the world, in action, promises, statements and in all our relationships. Complete truthfulness is indispensable to holiness. Romans 3:4 tells us that God is true and that if we want to be like Him we must be true too. We are to stand, 'having girded [our] loins with truth' (*Eph. 6:14*). Moreover, when the apostle tells us to think on 'whatever is true' he implies that we must reject what is untrue; we must beware of being carried away into an unreal world. We can try to escape the real world by withdrawing into our own world of imagination, a world of self-centred fantasy, creating an unreal life in our own minds, a life which God has not given us: we do this because we do not want to face up to our real world – the world He *has* given us. So many today are lured into an unreal world by means of drugs or alcohol which can lead only to suffering for themselves and those around them. In such cases, it is only the grace and truth of God that can deliver them. How much do we care about these people? How much do we think about them, pray for them, and seek to help them in a practical way?

Whatever is honourable, whatever is revered, highly respected, and worthy of regard. In 1 Timothy 3:11 the word is rendered 'grave': 'The women likewise must be serious, no slanderers, but temperate, faithful in all things.' In Titus 2:2 we read: 'Bid the older men be temperate, serious, sensible, sound in faith, in love, and in steadfastness'; 'In your teaching show integrity, gravity, and sound speech that cannot be censured, so that an opponent may be put to shame, having nothing evil to say of us' (*Tit. 2:7–8*). It does not express exactly what we mean today as honesty in our dealing with others, for example in business, but it expresses all behaviour that is worthy of a good reputation. The Christian is to esteem and respect all the laws and customs of society unless they are contrary to the law of God. Do our thoughts strengthen our view that man has been created in the image of God? Could we share our thoughts with the Lord Jesus? Paul is saying that if you want to know how to occupy your minds, think about what is honourable.

Whatever is just. This is the highest conception of what is right between man and man, a standard which would satisfy God and be worthy of His righteousness, to which we are meant to be conformed. Think of the world in which we live with all its craft and deceit, and you have the opposite of what is just and fair-minded. A Christian should be just in all his dealings. Non-Christians attach far more importance to the virtues of justice and honesty than they do to the regularity of a Christian's attendance at church meetings! If a Christian is to be a genuine example to the world he must show uncorrupted integrity in his dealings with other people in every sphere of his life. How much are we concerned about fairness in the society in which we live? Maybe as Christians we should spend less time nurturing each other and go into the rougher situations of life, seeking justice in a wider sphere such as members of councils and local committees where discussions are taking place and decisions are being made, seeking fair-mindedness and standards that would stand up in the presence of God.

Whatever is pure, what is morally undefiled, chaste in thought and deed. The Philippians were surrounded by pagan immorality, as we are surrounded by godless immorality today, and the apostle here is calling them as the children of God to a standard of sexual life which would be irreproachable. Today, in a society which has become openly and morally decadent, let us remember that as Christians the call and the standard set forth by the apostle is the standard laid down by the Lord Jesus Himself, the standard of God's purity. How do we as individuals face up to this? Do we make excuses and go along with the world, accepting their standards of sexual behaviour as just being modern and broad-minded? Do we accept sexual relationships in accordance with the permissive attitude towards sex which has pervaded our society, or do we esteem the purity of God as the standard for every Christian both in deed and in thought?

Whatever is lovely. This involves an attitude of mind which is gracious towards others and seeks to please them rather than ourselves. How can a Christian continue to be morose, irritable, bad-tempered, fault-finding, always impatient and insensitive to other people's feelings, and still think that he glorifies Jesus Christ? We are all prone to these weaknesses, but it is the attitude that we can justifiably *continue* in them without seeking to be changed which is wrong. There *is* grace to change us, just as there is grace to save us from sin in the first place.

Whatever is of good report, whatever is truly reputable. There are certain commendable virtues in the world which have existed in all ages and cultures – things like courtesy, respect for parents, for the old and for the disadvantaged. It is in upholding these standards that the Christian is a good example as a follower of Christ who Himself was always caring about other people. He should never be seen to be falling behind in any of these generally accepted social values if he is to be a valuable witness for Jesus Christ.

If there be any virtue, and if there be any praise, think on these things. The apostle did not say that this was a complete list of Christian virtues. He meant that if there is anything else that has true virtue the Christian should be showing it in his life. '*Nothing* that is of a contrary nature is right food for his thought.'[1] The apostle is telling the Philippians to study these virtues carefully, to reflect on them so that their lives may glorify Jesus Christ.

You can understand why it was that in the early Christian church the people said they could not live in the world and maintain this standard, so they became monks and nuns. That was not the purpose of what Paul was saying. What he *was* saying was that while we live in this world, we should

[1]William Hendriksen, *Philippians* (Edinburgh: Banner of Truth Trust, 1962), p. 199.

take steps to govern our thinking and remember that our thinking governs our actions. If what we think about does not come under these headings, we should put such things away and positively fill our minds with the things of God. This is the way to turn our thoughts from ourselves and from what pleases us. *The enemy of every Christian is ultimately his own selfishness*, his own natural disposition which always wants to turn his mind on to his own self, his own interests, his own troubles, his own problems, everything and anything to do with himself all the time. What the apostle is saying is, 'Open your minds to these other things – the good, lovely, pure, noble and high-minded things which are worthy of praise.'

Paul did not mean this to be an exercise in meditation on abstract theological ideas; he meant us to consider these virtues carefully and, as true followers of Jesus Christ, we are to practise them daily so that our lives have an influence on the world about us. Get into the habit of *not* thinking about yourself and your own interests only. Do not be overwhelmed by your own problems, sorrows and difficulties, but begin to think about God. Where are all these virtues wonderfully and gloriously summed up? The answer is in Jesus Christ. This is the call, to take our minds off ourselves, to take our minds off the godless ways in which the world thinks and acts, and to govern what we allow ourselves to think, what we allow ourselves to see, to read and so on, because all these things are going to affect our thought-life, and our thought-life affects our actions. What Paul is really saying to these Philippians is that all the things which are concerned with the Lord Jesus – they are the lovely, true, honourable, just, gracious and excellent things, the things which are full of praise, the things of God. How do we use our minds? What do we allow ourselves to think about, what is the company we keep, where do we go and what do we see? All these things affect our minds and the realm of thought in which we live. It is a great challenge to us all, but do not forget that this is God's world. He sent His Son into it in order that we should be changed, re-created after the image of God, and He sent His Holy Spirit into the world to enable us to live as the sons and daughters of God. What an opportunity there is to see this working out in our own lives!

9
Meditation and Self-Examination

What you have learned and received and heard and seen in me, do; and the God of peace will be with you. Philippians 4:9

We should read verse 8 again as a reminder. 'Finally, brethren, whatever is true, whatever is honourable, whatever is just, whatever is pure, whatever is lovely, whatever is gracious, if there is any excellence, if there is anything worthy of praise, think about these things. What you have learned and received and heard and seen in me, do; and the God of peace will be with you.'

We hear a great deal in these days about the mission of the church and, of course, it is vital that this should be very much in our minds, because the church that is not conscious of its mission in the world has lost its very breath of life. However, *one of the main factors in the success of the mission of the church, without any question, is the quality of life of the believers, of those who profess the Christian faith*. Paul, writing to these Philippians, had in mind the fact that he wanted them to be as the salt of the earth, as the light of the world. In other words, he wanted them to be conscious of their function in relation to other people, to those around them. He also realized that this function depended upon what they were in themselves as Christians, how much they really experienced of what they were preaching concerning the wonder and glory of the work of the Lord Jesus Christ. In writing to them in this alien situation in which they found themselves as Christians, surrounded by the heathen and permissive society in which they lived in Philippi, he was very concerned that their inner life – I have called it their thought-life – should be glorifying to God.

We have been considering our thought-life, its importance, its place in the plan of salvation and its subject matter, that is, whatever is true, honourable, just, pure, lovely, gracious. Paul told the Philippians to bear these things in mind; to *discipline* their minds to dwell on these things. He was concerned about the quality of their Christian life because in the end there ought to be a vast difference between *every* Christian and every non-Christian. The quality of our lives should be entirely and fundamentally different from that of non-Christians. Even here amongst us this morning, whether we like it or not, if we are Christians we should think in a particular way, in a God-orientated way, and live accordingly. If you are not a Christian then your whole way of thinking and looking at life is absolutely different. Paul was very concerned about these things, and that is why I have spent a little time going back over them. *The Lord Jesus has given us a particular quality of life, the life that God wants us to live in this world;* and the great question is, How does this really take hold of us, how do we enter into it more fully?

This next text presents another great challenge to all of us. Paul wrote to this Philippian church: 'Those things you have learned and received and heard and seen in me, *do*; and the God of peace will be with you.' The word 'received' is a technical word for handing on something you have received. Paul himself had received the things concerning the Christian faith, the things which were lovely, good and true and these were the things which he had handed on to the Philippians. Then he went on to say, 'and what you have seen in me'. These were not only the things about which they had heard him speak but, he told them, *they had actually seen these qualities in him*. In other words, he was setting himself up as an example. There are three parts to this text, and I want to look at it from the standpoint of all three: the example, the exhortation and the encouragements.

THE EXAMPLE

As I have already said, Paul set himself up as an example. He said, 'Those things which you have seen in me' – they were the things that were lovely, noble, true, gracious, full of excellence and praise. Now I can quite understand somebody here this morning thinking that this was rather a proud statement for the apostle Paul to make – to set *himself* up as an example of Christian living. Which of us would dare to say the same thing? I want to defend him by saying that not only was Paul a scholar in the school of Christ, but he was also a teacher, and all teachers should be good examples! He set himself up both as a teacher and as an example. Moreover, what we know about the apostle makes it quite clear that he was able to be this example because of the grace of God. He said that in Christ he could do all things. So we must read these words in the light of *all* his words: 'For to me to live is Christ, and to die is gain' (*Phil. 1:21*); 'For God is at work in you, both to will and to work for his good pleasure' (*Phil. 2:13*); 'For his sake I have suffered the loss of all things, and count them as refuse, in order that I may gain Christ and be found in him, not having a righteousness of my own, based on law, but that which is through faith in Christ, the righteousness from God that depends on faith' (*Phil. 3:8–9*). He said that it was by the grace of God that he was the man he was. This was his teaching. So when he set himself up as an example he was saying, 'If you want to see what Christ can do in a person, here it is in me.'

The point I am driving at is that Paul, whose life had been such an example to these Philippians, had been doing something which we so often neglect to do, and that is to examine ourselves – to spend some time in honest self-examination. He had stopped in his tracks, so to speak, and examined himself, and having done this he knew the changes which had taken place in him, wrought by the Holy Spirit bringing the life of Christ into him. It was not his old nature being improved, but a new nature, the nature of Jesus Christ which was growing in him. He said he was a different man from Saul on the road to Damascus.

This leads me to digress for a short while to talk about something which is very rarely mentioned these days, and that is self-examination as part of the Christian life. I do this for some very important reasons.

1. This is the way in which we become acquainted with ourselves. Unless we look at our lives, our thought-life, what occupies our minds, we do not become aware of what we really are, what our character is, where our hearts lie. It is not enough just to hear the Word of God. Many people hear it but it does not make any difference to them because they never take it and compare themselves with what it is they have heard from it. We must make the Word of God our own by comparing ourselves with the standards that God has set us as Christians, and then we will begin to uncover what we really are, our motives, which are often very subtle. We may do something which outwardly appears to be good and very commendable, but inwardly all that we are looking for is praise of men and not the praise and glory of God and the extension of His kingdom. So unless we examine ourselves we do not uncover our secret desires, our hidden attitudes and prejudices. There are habits and weaknesses which we have got to face and ask ourselves, 'What is the truth about me?' This is a very hard thing to do; it is not a popular teaching but it is the only way in which we will actually come nearer to knowing ourselves as God knows us.

2. I want to go further and say that it is only by means of self-examination that a sinner becomes aware of the fact that he *is* a sinner. The trouble today is that people do not want to examine themselves, but this is how a sinner becomes conscious of his guilt before God. This is how he begins to see the strength of the evil desires which are within him and the inclinations of his heart which are against God and the things of God. This is how, in fact, he begins to see the hardness of his heart which makes him want to hold on to his sin instead of allowing God to break into his life and change it. Left to himself, man always wants to persist in the way of disobedience, he wants to live his own life, whatever God has said or revealed about Himself. It is only when he begins to see all these inclinations as sin existing and operating in his own heart that he realizes that when God condemns sin He is just in His condemnation. Unless a sinner comes to this place, any profession of conversion is purely superficial, and it is only when, by the grace of God, he becomes convicted of his sin that he wants to turn to the Lord Jesus Christ for the remedy.

3. Moreover, it is by self-examination that the Christian comes to know the reality of his Christian experience. As in the case of Paul, he sees the change that has taken place in himself; he knows that there is something in him that must always bring him back to God, even though at times he may want to rebel against Him. You and I know this and it is a sign that we belong to God. When we do wrong we have a consciousness of guilt, a sadness about our sin, and in the end we *have* to come back to Him for forgiveness because we know that we have trespassed against the love and mercy of God towards us. Ultimately, we find that we love the things that belong to God, the people of God and the worship of God. When we meet people who love the Lord Jesus, there is an affinity between us; we know that they are 'our people'. More and more a Christian has an assurance in his own heart

that God has changed him and is changing him and, as John said, 'If our hearts do not condemn us, we have confidence before God' (*1 John 3:21*).

4. Not only is self-examination the means by which we understand what has happened to us spiritually, but it is an essential condition in preparing us to turn from our own sinfulness to a love of holiness and to grow in holiness. When a Christian examines himself in the light of the Word of God he sees the sinfulness and weakness of his own nature and his need for grace. This is what makes him come back to God and say, 'Lord, I have got this evil desire in my heart; I even love the things I should not love. Please take them away from me because I want to love the things that belong to You and not the things that hurt You.' Unless we examine ourselves like this, the Word of God only passes into our minds and passes out again; it does not really affect us. I say it advisedly and carefully that the Bible is absolutely clear that self-examination alongside the Scriptures is one of the chief ways by which the Holy Spirit enables us to see the need for our natures to be changed and transformed into the likeness of Jesus Christ. I hear a great deal in these days about the gifts of the Holy Spirit, but very little about self-examination and the *fruit* of the Holy Spirit which means holiness. It is in seeing the very sinfulness of our natures, even as Christians, and our need for holiness, that makes us cry to God, 'Lord, by Your Spirit come and change us so that we love the things that You love and hate the things that You hate. Come and fill our lives.'

5. Self-examination is also obviously essential in the whole question of the discipline of our thought-life or self-government, if you like, and the peace of mind and the joy which come to the man or woman who is self-disciplined. We cannot be at peace with God if we know that we have been disobedient. The person who is not at peace with himself cannot be at peace with God. When Paul said, 'For me to live

is Christ', he knew that this was true; he had nothing to fear, he was like an open book before God, he was willing to be searched by Him. Although he was in prison, chained to soldiers and under the sentence of death, he knew that his life was in the hands of the Lord Jesus Christ and he knew the peace of God. Paul practised self-examination, and Christ had so mastered his thoughts that he could appeal to the Philippians to remember that this was exemplified in his life, in his speech and in his deeds. It is very important to realize that we are God's people and that *the more disciplined our thought-life is the more His peace will fill our hearts and minds.*

THE EXHORTATION

Now let us move on rather quickly to the exhortation. Paul said, 'What you have learned and heard and seen in me, *do*.' In other words, live out these things in your own lives. But if we really are going to put them into practice in our relationships with other people, we must realize that our actions are only the outward expression of our thoughts. It is our thoughts which are the source and ruler of our actions; they make us what we are. As Bishop Steere wrote, 'We are two men, each of us – what is seen and what is not seen. But *the unseen is the maker of the other*.' So if we would *do* these things, the true, honourable, just, pure, lovely and gracious, then these are the things which must fill our minds. Indeed, we must make a habit of thinking about them, and habits are made only by repetition, by habitually rejecting the wrong thoughts and fostering the right ones. It is the habit of right thinking that is the foundation of a life made up of the right actions.

But I want to mention another aspect of our thought-life which is very rarely spoken about these days. It is the place of meditation in our lives, the definite concentration of the mind on these spiritually uplifting matters. I know we live in an age when everybody is rushing, and you may think you are far too busy to meditate. I agree with you – you are too busy! I remember an incident concerning George Müller and Dr Barnardo which happened many years ago. In an amazing and wonderful way, Dr Barnardo was helping to save children by running a very large home for them, and he was exceedingly busy travelling up and down the country urging people to give to this very worthy and needy cause. But in doing so he was wearing himself out, so he came to see George Müller, who was maintaining a home for hundreds of children too; indeed he was also responsible for the support of 120 missionaries on the field. Müller travelled all over the world telling people of his experience of God's faithfulness, but he never spoke to anybody about the needs of the orphans as far as raising money was concerned. He dealt only with God. He was a man who, with all his responsibilities – and they were very great indeed – still found time to spend hours in prayer, and he was a man of great peace. So it was to him that Dr Barnardo turned when he needed help to cope with his great work and yet remain in good health. George Müller's strength came from the time he spent with God.

We have been considering some of the greatest truths the human mind can consider, but how can these great truths become part of us? If it is only by thinking about them for the very short time we have on a Sunday, then it is woe betide us all. However busy we are we need to find time to pray, to read our Bibles and to think about these great eternal truths; to meditate upon them, to examine them in our own minds, and then, I believe, they will become part and parcel of our whole beings. Most people today lead very busy lives; the pace of life has quickened tremendously, and for most of us it is not possible to spend hours a day in meditation, but that does not mean that we can neglect it completely. However demanding our lives may be as Christian people we must find some time each day to read God's Word, to pray and to meditate upon God, however limited that time may be. These are as essential ingredients to our spiritual life as food, drink and sleep are to our natural lives. Without them we become stunted Christians and will lose the peace of God from our lives. Let us remember that it is these eternal things which will remain when all the business of our lives is past, however important and demanding it may seem to us today.

It is in meditating that we begin to *feel* the weight of the truths about God, and through our minds they begin to affect our hearts and lives. Richard Baxter said, 'Great truths will do great work upon the heart.' You see, there is nothing automatic in spiritual things; we do not automatically grow in spiritual matters. What we sow in the realm of the Spirit of God we will also reap, and meditation is a way of sowing, because it is our thoughts and feelings which move our wills to action. How did people write the Psalms and the wonderful hymns we sing? 'Jesus, the very thought of Thee/ With sweetness fills my breast'; 'How sweet the Name of Jesus sounds/In a believer's ear'; 'When I survey the wondrous Cross/On which the Prince of glory died'. Where did they get these words from? They came because these people meditated, they considered, they thought of the wonderful things that God had prepared for them. They thought about the Lord Jesus Christ, His love and His death for them. They found time to do these things. It is regular meditation that results in the right habits of thinking, meditation upon the Scriptures, sermons, Christian books, the things we read of in verse 8, meditation upon the things of God, the things which bring peace and joy to our minds and hearts. 'On this mountain the Lord of hosts will make for all peoples a feast of good things' (*Isa. 25:6*). God wants us to be so full of these great truths that we feel we are feasting on good things, the things of God.

People think that self-examination is a bore, and they confuse it with negative introspection, the uncovering of sin and weakness, or being concerned only with our problems. Oh no, this is not a negative thing. We are not spending time dwelling upon our weaknesses and inability to do anything about them and then becoming thoroughly depressed. We are uncovering the grace of God within our lives; we are concerned with the *great* things that God has done for us in the past and what He will do for us in the future; we want to fill our minds with these things. Let me again quote Richard Baxter to you. He said, 'When you meditate on any Scripture truth, think of it as a beam of eternal light from heaven; indited by the Holy Spirit to lead men to obedience and felicity: behold it with reverence as a letter or message sent from heaven: and as a thing of grand importance to your souls. When you meditate upon any grace, think of it as part of the image of God, implanted and actuated by the Holy Spirit to advance the soul into communion with God and to prepare it for him . . . *Take in God if you would feel life and power in all that you meditate on.*'

Here I would bring one more point before you. If necessary we have got to preach a sermon to ourselves. I believe this is what Paul meant when he said, '*Do* these things'. If our lives are to be of the right quality we have got to spend more time seriously with God, we must be aware of the way we are thinking about spiritual things, and then we will find our hearts full to overflowing with the good, the joyful, the wonderful things of God. This will result in the right actions: we will 'do these things' which are honourable, just, pure, lovely, gracious and excellent. There is here not only an example before us, the great example of the apostle Paul, but there is also the great exhortation to spend time to fill our minds with the things of God. Whereas God is to be in our thoughts at all times, yet it is imperative to set aside time on our own to meditate upon these truths, to read books which help us to understand them, to pray over them, to share them with God.

THE ENCOURAGEMENTS

Let me close with two encouragements.

1. We have the Bible, so we have plenty on which to meditate. It is full of the great truths of the gospel, whereas the Philippians probably had very little. They had Paul's letter, probably one letter among the whole church and only a few copies of the Gospels (if they were written by then). There may have been a few leaders in their church who were beginning to help them, but they did not have all the help that we have today. Paul was their bible; he told them, 'Learn from my life'. *You may be the only bible that people around you are reading, and it is when they see your life that they are confronted with God because of His work in you.* I hope and pray that the message will be clear in all of us. Paul wanted this great responsibility and privilege to be the experience of the Philippians, and it should be ours as well.

2. Finally, Paul told these Philippians that if they did these things, 'the God of peace will be with you'. This was not just the peace of God but God in His being, *as the source of tranquillity*, who would be in their lives. He would bring with Him the peace that He has in Himself – in life, in prison, in death. Remember what David said: 'Though I walk through the valley of the shadow of death, I will fear no evil.' Why? 'For *thou* art with me.' You will know what David knew – God's peace which passes all understanding and which is given to us. God, the God of peace, will be with you when you fill your hearts and minds with these great truths concerning His gospel, the gospel of Jesus Christ our Lord. Let us learn to walk in the footsteps of this servant of Christ and know the fruits of our Lord's saving power. May God help us to take these things seriously and fill our lives with the good things of God.

10

Learning to Be Content

Not that I complain of want; for I have learned, in whatever state I am, to be content. I know how to be abased, and I know how to abound; in any and all circumstances I have learned the secret of facing plenty and hunger, abundance and want.

Philippians 4:11–12

You will remember that one of the reasons why Paul wrote this letter to the church at Philippi was to thank them for the gift of money they had sent to him by the hand of Epaphroditus. In verse 10 he said, 'I rejoice in the Lord greatly that now at length you have revived your concern for me: you were indeed concerned for me, but you had no opportunity.' I will return to this verse later on when dealing with verses 14–18. Just now I want to be concerned with verse 11, which strikes at the heart of every one of us because it deals with this matter of contentment – learning to be content. Although refreshed and encouraged by the generosity of the Philippians, the apostle goes on to tell them that what he says to them has not been dictated by his wants; in other words, he has not been in a state of discontent in prison because, he says, 'I have learned in whatever circumstance I am, to be content.' That is the connection. Let us remind ourselves again that he was in prison, probably suffering from cold and damp; he was an old warrior of Christ, facing a death sentence; he was also lonely, cut off from the church, the people whom he loved, yet in *these* circumstances he could testify that he was content – not of himself (verse 13 makes that quite clear) *but through Christ alone*. He says, 'I can do all things *in him*' – in Christ – 'who strengthens me.' So you can see that here is a man of God who had reached the stage where, *despite his circumstances, contentment was his frame of mind*.

The question facing me, and I trust facing us all, is, 'How do we come to this state of contentment?' You may think that Paul was a special person because he was an apostle, but this was not so and this is not the way in which we must consider him because, in fact, God has told us that He is no respecter of persons. *He has also promised that in whatever situation He places us there will be grace to deal with it;* so we must not make Paul a special case. God is equally the Father of us all, so we are without excuse. Let us therefore look carefully at the way in which Paul found the grace of Jesus Christ and how that grace could and *did* bring him to this place of contentment. After all, we live in a discontented age and, too often, the spirit of discontent permeates the church, the body of Christ, which is a shame to us and dishonouring to Him. It is easy to think that we would be content if only our situation were different; we delude ourselves into thinking that it is our circumstances which need to be changed and not ourselves! What God wants to do is to *change us* so that we learn to be content with our present circumstances, and it is when He changes us that we learn to be content with them; *this* is how our lives glorify Him. In studying this verse it is important for us to see exactly what Paul is saying and to learn to apply it to ourselves.

THE SCHOOL OF LIFE – 'I HAVE LEARNED'

The apostle said, 'Not that I complain of want; for I have learned' – *I have learned*. So we begin by seeing that, in explaining the reason why he is in this condition, he is reminding the Philippians that this is not something that has come about by chance, it is not some fortuitous combination of circumstances which has brought about this state of mind, it is not something that has come about by nature. I know some people are more content than others, some are more placid; others, by nature, are more restless and discontented. But even the best of natures breaks down if a situation becomes unbearable, and it would break down in such circumstances as those in which Paul found himself. At the end of his life, after a period of great service and much suffering in the cause of Christ, what is his reward? It was a prison and a death sentence. *How* could he be content? *How* can you be content when you have been treated unfairly, when you are lonely or disappointed, when things in your personal life or career have gone wrong? However placid or content you may be by nature, it seems that there are circumstances which go beyond anything in which it is reasonable for us to remain content. I want to remind you, too, that this is not necessarily anything to do with educational attainment. So often we think of the word 'learning' in connection with normal educational processes but Paul is not referring to this type of learning. In fact, you may be highly educated according to worldly standards and yet be in the kindergarten of this particular learning. On the other hand, you may be a person who is unlearned by the world's standards and yet, if I may use the analogy, you may be a professor in this school of learning because it is not an ordinary school and it is not concerned with ordinary learning: this is the school of Christ. Let us consider this word 'learning' in more detail.

1. The apostle says, 'I have learned', and the implication is very clear. He has not come to this position easily or quickly; this spiritual learning is a *process*. It has come about as a result of years of experience, as indeed in the natural

realm. To master a subject takes many years of study, often spread over a long period of time, even a lifetime, and Paul is saying that he had to learn this spiritual lesson of contentment; it had been a process in the school of life; there had been repeated lessons. So when people say they have had an instantaneous religious experience in Christian matters which, they claim, has suddenly enabled them to be completely content and remain in that state, this is not true.

2. This spiritual learning is also a *progression*; as in the ordinary process of learning, you go from one stage to another. In His mercy, God often gives us the simpler lessons at the beginning and the harder ones as we go on. All the time we should be making progress, learning daily to be content with all the circumstances of our lives. But, let us be perfectly honest, there is not one of us, who has been in this school, who has not said at times, 'I have failed.' When as children we attended school we were given problems to solve and, unfortunately, we were not always able to deal with them; we failed and got things wrong sometimes. The same is true spiritually; we find ourselves in a state of murmuring and complaining – the very thing that Paul says he does not do. We have failed to solve the problem, we have failed to pass the test. There were times also when we were children when we were rebuked for wrong-doing, and the same is true spiritually. God rebukes us; we have a sense of having lost His presence and we are unhappy. Indeed, at times, God can even take stronger steps to deal with us, He chastises us in one way or another. But many people refuse to see it is *God* who is chastising them, and they miss so much of the meaning of their Christian life; they put down their situations to every other cause but that it is *God* who is dealing with them in this school of learning. Moreover, as in natural learning, when the basic principles have been learned, that knowledge has to be continually applied to new circumstances as they occur in our lives. In this verse Paul is saying

that he has learned something and this learning has been as a result of a schooling in the things of God.

3. There is no genuine educational progress without *discipline*. Now I know that schooling for young children today has been made as much like play as possible, because this is the way in which educationalists believe they learn, but in the end there has to be work as well. There are times when a child's mind has to be trained and disciplined, and there are no short cuts. Today, as some of you may know, there is beginning to be a swing in education back to greater discipline – sometimes it seems to me that it is very slow in coming. And, of course, the same thing applies in this school, there is a *discipline of God*; He calls us to exercise our gifts, our determination, courage, and, if necessary, to deny ourselves and put aside pleasure as the first aim of our lives. You may say, 'This is not a very encouraging sort of gospel that you are preaching', but I am being realistic, I am being honest about the things of God. You remember that the psalmist David said that God disciplined him; he bore the yoke in his youth. And Asaph, one of the most godly men, said that he had been corrected by God (*Ps. 73*). If we think that the Christian life is not a school we are missing an understanding of what God is doing with us; it is a process, a progression, and it is a discipline.

4. It is a *meaningful activity*. Surely when we send our children to school we believe that they are involved in something which is meaningful, that they are being equipped for life. Paul is saying that in this school God has been working His purpose out; it has not been something haphazard; there has been a meaningful, purposeful controlling of his life in order that at the end of it he could say, 'I have learned'. He had learned one of the great lessons – he had learned to be content. After all, is this not a most wonderful thing to be? Let us look at this man again: he is coming towards the end of his life; he is in prison, writing

this letter in which he has been talking about rejoicing, as well as all the other great and glorious things we have considered. His learning had been directed to the end that even in prison, facing death, he was at peace, content with what God had allowed for him. Can we say that we have reached this stage of contentment?

5. It is imperative that we see our Christian life from the standpoint of being in the school of Christ – learning to be more like Him *all* the time. This has an immense significance because it means that *the Christian life is never meaningless*. However mundane our lives may appear to be from the outside, inwardly there is a ceaseless spiritual activity in which we are involved every day and all day, and there is always room for progress to apply what we have learned and to glorify God in our lives. As we grow older life does not take a downward path but an upward one. Paul said that 'though our outward man perish, yet the inward man is renewed day by day' (*2 Cor. 4:16*). He said, 'I know how to be abased, and I know how to abound; in any and all circumstances I have learned to be content' – he had learned the secret. There is an element of the mysterious; it is a secret work of the Spirit of God, and this is why the work of the Holy Spirit is not altogether open to natural intellectual analysis.

THE SCHOOL'S CURRICULUM

Well, now, let us consider for ourselves the school of Christ. What is the curriculum, what happens there, what is the variety of subjects? It seems to me that in this verse, Paul sets that curriculum before us. He is saying that the overall lesson is a doctrinal one – *God allows His children to experience life in a variety of circumstances*. He says, 'I have learned, in whatever state I am, to be content. I know how to be abased, and I know how to abound.' He had learned the secret of facing plenty and want. It is not easy to be deprived of the natural and normal satisfactions of life; it is particularly difficult to be in want and yet to be content. He knew what it meant to be brought low in health, in reputation, times when people rejected him, when he was under great pressure. What about the hunger and thirst that must have possessed him? Remember what he wrote in 2 Corinthians. At times he felt as if the sentence of death was upon Him. He was pressed beyond measure, he despaired of life, and they had to rush him out of the city like a criminal, pursued from one town to another as he was being persecuted. He knew what it was to be hunted like an outlaw, like a reject of society, and even his own countrymen wanted to stone him to death. He said he had been in *all* these circumstances but, at the same time, he said, 'I know not only how to be abased, I know how to abound – I have learned to live in that situation too.' You can make a list – temptation, trial, persecution, success, opposition, lack of fellowship, loneliness, good health, poor health, freedom, imprisonment, hardship, disappointments, comforts and joys. In effect, Paul said, 'Put them all together, this is what I have been through, these are the basic ingredients of the school in which I have been, but I found God teaching me in these things. In all these different problems that God sent to me I have learned from the discipline of this school of God.' On the other hand, there are times when it seems to be just the opposite, when everything prospers, our health is in a good state, work is there, money is coming in, there are friends, family, spiritual blessing; everything is going well. Let us remind ourselves that it *is* a school, the curriculum *is* varied, all these things are the basic ingredients of the school programme, but *it is God's school and He is in charge*.

LESSONS TO BE LEARNED IN THE SCHOOL OF GOD

This leads me on to ask the question, 'What is behind the curriculum?' What are the aims? First of all, we must realize that the aims of the school are good and beneficial. God wants us to learn to trust Him, to live in His constant love, and to be like Him, to live lives which glorify Him and help to extend His kingdom. *He wants us to learn through every circumstance in life that His purpose for us is good*, that His love for us is constant, and that it is not dependent upon any circumstances in which we may find ourselves in this world, however hard they may be.

There are lessons to be learned through the changes in our circumstances.

1. *They encourage the people of God to go back and seek His grace and to live in dependence on Him*. This means that we are bringing God into our lives every day and all day so that every part of our lives is being orientated towards Him. This is what life is all about – living in the right relationship to God. Apart from these circumstances, so often we would forget God, we would become too materialistic, too wedded to the security of the people around us and the things of this world. You may think that this is not so, but let us remember that the Bible tells us that even some of the men of God – David, for instance, in his prosperity, forgot God; Solomon with his unsurpassable wisdom, forgot God. On the other hand, Elijah, in his great need in the desert, had to trust God for food, and deliverance came to him through the poverty of a widow's home; he was utterly dependent on God alone. Paul had to trust God for the safety of his own life and the lives of the others on board the ship in which he sailed, and they were rescued. Our Lord's greatest mission was carried out with a few fishermen as His disciples. Amidst all His suffering, He endured and could say to His Father, 'If it seems good in thy sight'. So God uses all circumstances in life to keep us turning to Himself, realizing that our only security is to be found in Him, seeking His grace to live *in faith*, not just blind faith but complete trust in God's faithfulness as revealed in His Word.

2. The second lesson to be learned in this school is that *God's goodness and love towards us do not change*. He tests us, if you like, to see whether we are fair-weather Christians because He wants us to learn about His faithfulness in *all* circumstances. This is what lies behind the Book of Job. How was it possible that a man in Job's condition could be in favour with God? The fact is that he *was* in favour with God. Even when he was covered with boils and in sackcloth and ashes, even when his own mind was in turmoil about his circumstances, God was looking after him, and God was upon him and never forsook him for one moment. When Job saw God, the great, everlasting, unchangeable and eternal God he said, 'Now my eye sees thee; therefore I despise myself, and repent in dust and ashes' (*Job 42:5–6*).

3. In all the variety of our circumstances *God teaches us the truth about ourselves*. He shows us the evil that is within our hearts and our weakness so that He can deal with them. All of us have fallen natures, we are born 'of the flesh', as our Lord said to Nicodemus, so that even after we are converted, born anew, born of the Spirit, we will retain sinful natures which need to be changed, and this is a lengthy process. In a variety of circumstances, our sinfulness, pride, selfishness, self-indulgence and lack of control, self-centredness and self-pity, all lie deep within us, and often we try to ignore them in ourselves and to hide them from other people by a superficial veneer of reasonable behaviour. In adversity there is also the temptation to be covetous and jealous of others, even other Christians who are not afflicted in the same way as ourselves. In poverty a spirit of bitterness can take hold of us so that we murmur against God and even resort to wrong means of changing our condition, as the servant of Elisha did. On the other hand, the danger of wealth is that it becomes easy to depend upon it and the freedom which often comes with it, so that we are lulled into a false security and become too materialistic and careless of a sense of God.

Ultimately we are driven back to the great fundamental truths which are the foundation of our Christian life. Throughout the Bible God reveals Himself to us as the Creator and Ruler of this world, but He has also revealed Himself as the Father of mankind in general and more particularly of His own people, His chosen ones. What did he say to Pharaoh? 'Thus says the Lord, Israel is my first-born son, and I say to you, "Let my son go that he may serve me"' (*Exod. 4:23*). In the wilderness Moses reminded the children of Israel, 'Is not he your father, who created you, who made you and established you?' (*Deut. 32:6*). Many years later Isaiah prayed, 'Yet, O Lord, thou art our Father; we are the clay, and thou art our potter; we are all the work of thy hand' (*Isa. 64:8*). Then when we turn to the New Testament we see that during His ministry, (time and time again) our Lord referred to God as His Father: 'No one comes to the Father, but by me' (*John 14:6*); 'I am in the Father and the Father in me' (*John 14:11*); 'Father, the hour has come; glorify thy Son that the Son may glorify thee' (*John 17:1*). But He also told the disciples, 'I am ascending to *my* Father and *your* Father, to *my* God and *your* God' (*John 20:17*). In Matthew chapter 6 we read how He taught His disciples that great family prayer, '*Our* Father who art in heaven . . .', and later in the same chapter He told them, 'Do not be anxious about your life, what you shall eat or what you shall drink, nor about your body, what you shall put on . . . Look at the birds of the air: they neither sow nor reap nor gather into barns, and yet your heavenly Father feeds them. Are you not of more value than they? . . . Therefore do not be anxious . . . your heavenly Father knows that you need them all.' It is the same wonderful message of the apostle in Romans, chapter 8: 'For you did not receive the spirit of slavery to fall back into fear, but you have received the *spirit of sonship*.' Or again, 'All things work together for good to those who love God, to those who are called according to His purpose.' He has called us,

He is our Father, we are His children, and no circumstances can ever alter our eternal relationship to Him. We have been adopted into His family through Jesus Christ. He is the One who is in control of *all* the circumstances of our lives and nothing can overtake us which He does not allow for our good. Even the devil with all his wiles can never change our status as the children of God, nor can he ever pluck us out of His hand; we are there eternally.

Then there is the cross of Jesus Christ which is the pledge of His love for us. Every day we can lift our eyes to God and whatever else we cannot say we *can* say, 'O God, my Father, You loved us so much that You sent Your Son into the world to die for us so that we might be forgiven and restored into Your presence.' Every day we can say, 'O God, we know something of Your merciful love towards us; when we did not deserve anything You freely forgave us.' Every day every Christian can go back to God and say, 'I *know*, O God, that You love me in Jesus Christ so much that through Him You reconciled me to Yourself. I *know* that You love me not only for time but for eternity; You have given me eternal life through Jesus Christ my Lord.' So all the time God is making us live in the light of the Fatherhood of God, in the light of the Cross of Jesus Christ and all that it means.

The third great truth is the indwelling of the Holy Spirit to enable us to live this life. He alone is the One who enlightens, convicts, and transforms us and enables us to live as the children of God. This spiritual activity is not part of our natural birth, it is not generated by anything within our own hearts, it is only the Holy Spirit who imparts His spiritual life to us. Moreover, as the children of God there is the certain pledge and promise that the work that He has begun He will complete. 'He who has begun a good work in you will bring it to completion at the day of Jesus Christ' (*Phil. 1:6*). He has promised us His sanctifying love and regenerating power in life and, whatever the circumstances, God's promise concerning the work of the Holy Spirit in us will never fail. This is the meaning of holiness and mortification, where the 'old man' is put to death daily; but it is also the school of *life*, the school of love and *eternal life*. Let us not quarrel with our Lord's provisions; rather let the love of Christ teach us to grow in grace and so to enter that peace of contentment founded upon the love of God the Father, the love of Christ crucified, and the purifying love of God the Holy Spirit.

11
'I Can Do All Things in Him Who Strengthens Me'

'I can do all things in him who strengthens me'. Philippians 4:13

This text is the climax of verses 11–12, where the apostle Paul shared with us his experience in the school of Christ, where he learned the lesson of contentment. This final statement is his testimony, his examination result – 'I can do all things in him who strengthens [or empowers] me.'

Well, what a testimony! And let us not forget as we look at it together that Paul was a man of like passions as ourselves. He too was a sinner saved by the grace of the Lord Jesus Christ, with a nature distorted by sin, subject to all sorts of pressures and persecutions, loneliness, rejection, opposition, his body subject to weaknesses, to disease and the infirmities of old age, just like everybody else. We have a tendency to put the apostles in a category of being very special people who did not have the same temptations and trials as we have, but this really is a let-out for ourselves. Paul was writing to this Philippian church from a Roman prison under the possible sentence of death, every movement limited by chains, and yet he still wrote, 'I can do all things in him who strengthens [or empowers] me.'

'I CAN DO ALL THINGS'

The first obvious thing to say about this is that if you take these words as they stand they are obviously not true, are they? This is a good example of the way in which the Bible must *not* be used. When people say, 'I can do all things through Christ', *can* they? Could the apostle Paul? I do not think he could. For instance, he could not release himself from this prison. He could not strike off those chains in the way the angel struck off the chains when Peter was in prison. He could not get rid of the 'thorn in the flesh' which God had given him. What did he mean then when he said these words? As I have already said, this is a good example of how the Bible should be read and how it should *not* be read. It should not be read by merely taking a single promise, a statement, or even the testimony of the apostle, out of its context. I am sure there are many students who when facing examinations say, 'I wish through Christ all of us could get a "first"'! You cannot do it, much as you would like to. Christian or non-Christian, unless the work has been done and God has given you the ability to get a 'first'. Well, what did the apostle mean? The truth is that we must read the Bible in its context; we must read the passage in the light of the meaning of the words or statements that surround it. In this passage Paul had been dealing with the question of living in a variety of circumstances – hunger, poverty, abundance and want, and this verse really is the climax of this passage: 'I have learned the secret of facing plenty, hunger, abundance and want, I can do all things in him who strengthens me.' He said he was able to live in contentment as a child of God, in peace and fellowship with God, carrying out God's purposes for his life in all the circumstances in which it had pleased God to place him. Whatever the temptations, whatever the trials, pressures of body or mind, whatever the afflictions, even prosperity and success, with all the temptations that surround them, whether he was in a damp cell chained to a Roman centurion or whether he was on the Mediterranean Sea, he had learned in all these situations that through Christ he could carry out the purposes of God and live as His child in them all. That is really what he was saying.

What an example! And, indeed, what a challenge if this is what God *can* do in the lives of the children of God! We must ask ourselves how far we have grown, how much we have learned in the school of Christ. What a rebuke to our murmurings, our grumbles, our discontent, our fears, our dissatisfactions, and our disappointments with God's provisions for us, we who have so much to help us. After all, humanly speaking, Paul could have said, 'O God, I have served You for these past years, I have been persecuted, I have got the marks of the lashes on my back, I have got this thorn in the flesh and the reward I get for these years of devoted labour is that I find myself under a sentence of death in a Roman prison, chained to soldiers. Where is the eventide of my life with its tranquillity, its peace, its sunshine, its pleasantness and its comfort?' Instead, he said, '*I am rejoicing in God*, I have learned, in whatever state I am, to be content.' So this man is a great man, a great Christian man, and God has set him before us as an example of what can happen to us in the grace of the Lord Jesus Christ.

WHY DO WE FAIL?

We have looked at Paul's testimony and the meaning of his words, 'I can do all things through Christ', but let us ask the practical question, 'Why do we fail?' It is easy to read these words, to be impressed by them and, at times, to rejoice in them because we feel that, like Paul, we are riding on the crest of the wave. Paul was saying that he could do all things, whatever the circumstances. Why do we fail? In my preparation I was trying to think seriously as to *why* we fail and I have got various suggestions.

1. Firstly, I believe, in these days there is a fundamental misunderstanding of what Christianity is all about. So many Christians, and especially young Christians, believe that there is something automatic about the Christian life, and I regret that this is often the impression that has been given to them by older Christians. They believe that the moment they accept the Lord Jesus Christ everything in life is going to be wonderful; like the weeds that seem to grow in our gardens without any effort, they do not have problems, they just grow! But there is nothing automatic in spiritual things; God never sees us as a computer or a machine in which, the moment you press the button, certain processes must follow.

2. As far as our misunderstanding is concerned we have also got the idea that somehow or other we can get on, shall I say, half-heartedly. This is what Bonhoeffer called 'cheap grace'. We believe that all we need is a little time in prayer, occasional Bible study here and there, church-going, maybe the occasional prayer meeting if we have a free evening, even perhaps coming to Communion, and with a few good deeds done in a pleasant manner, taking everything in our stride. We think that if we follow this pattern everything will be all right, and we will reach this stage of being like the apostle – living in victory. But it is a very half-hearted matter – so much, no further. It is 'cheap grace'. It does not work that way. That is not the way the Bible teaches us, as we shall see in a moment.

3. I think the other misunderstanding is that some Christians think that unless we give the impression to everybody around us that the Christian life is like a long holiday, then we are failing, we are dishonouring God. I think this is a serious mistake because if you had seen the apostle at certain times you would have realized that for him the Christian life was *not* a holiday. He was persecuted,

afflicted; people were jealous of him and we find that, at times, he was cast out, some people in the church even hated him. There were times when he himself was hard-pressed, and maybe you would have found him on his knees, beseeching God to take away these afflictions from him. You would not have found, in any sense of the word, that the Christian life for him was easy and that he always went about with a smile. Do not forget that the Lord Jesus Christ Himself was 'a man of sorrows and acquainted with grief', and the paradox of this strange and inexplicable mystery of the Christian life is that *despite* the experience of trials and temptations there is an underlying peace, there is an underlying joy, *but it does not come automatically*. I believe that so often we fail to find this peace and joy because we have a wrong concept of the Christian life; we put up a front for other people to see and it is this front which concerns us instead of the reality – that is, what God is doing with us.

4. I also believe that we fail so often because we do not wrestle with God over our reactions to His will and purpose for us. We must realize that in the school of faith God is always calling on us to grow – to apply our faith afresh. It is not enough to say, 'I am saved, I believe in the Lord Jesus Christ', and then grumble like the unregenerate. That is not the Christian life as we see it in the Bible. We have got to recognize that there are times in our lives when there is a fundamental clash between what I believe God *ought* to give me and what God actually *does* give me, and the two things may be very different. There has to be a reconciliation, a real bending and breaking of my own will to accept the will of God; there has to be a conflict and the first thing we have to do is to *recognize* that there is this conflict between our wills and the will of God. Then we must go back to God about this conflict and say to Him, as Job said to Him, 'I do not understand You.' What is more, we have got to *deal with God* concerning this conflict. We must *seek* for a change of heart,

we must seek strength from the Word of God and we must pray about it. Unless we are seriously concerned about the conflict between our will and God's will for us, I do not believe we will ever enter into that peace that Paul knew when he said, 'I can do all things through him who strengthens [or empowers] me.'

'CHRIST WHO EMPOWERS ME'

When the apostle said, 'I can do all things through him who strengthens [or empowers] me', he was saying that this was not a natural gift with which he was born, this was not a characteristic of his personality. He was aware that this came from the Lord Jesus Christ – 'I can do all things *in him*'. The source of his enabling, the One who empowered him, who strengthened him, was the Lord Jesus Christ. He was not looking at himself or his own resources but he was looking entirely to the Lord Jesus to enable him *daily* to live in victory. This immediately takes us right into the *realm of God*. Here was a man who believed that while he was going about the streets of Rome, while he was preaching, living on a ship which was bringing him to Rome, traversing the mountains as a missionary pilgrim, while he was in prison facing a death sentence, he was constantly aware that what he did, he did through the strength of Christ; that *it was God*, the eternal, the everlasting, the almighty God who was empowering him. The real thing that we are up against, as we shall see in a moment, is unbelief. *Do I really believe that God actually empowers me*? Paul believed that the resources of Jesus Christ could and would be given to him day by day.

How could he believe this? He could believe it because his faith was based on what he knew to be true concerning the new birth, that he was a new creature and that God had supernaturally given him powers which he did not possess before, new desires, new resources, a new vision, that he was a new man in Jesus Christ, that through the Holy Spirit God had given him the potential to live as a child of God. He believed that when he came to Christ he was born anew and when he saw his own weakness he did not despair. He said, 'I will all the more gladly boast of my weaknesses, that the power of Christ may rest upon me . . . for when I am weak, then I am strong' (*2 Cor. 12:9–10*). He was born again, so when he saw his natural weaknesses *he went back to God* to give him His resources, to give him power. Because he knew he was a new creature in Christ he also knew that by the enabling of God's Spirit these resources could grow in him. I wonder if we go back to God about our own weaknesses, based upon the new birth, regeneration, call it what you like.

The third thing is that the *Holy Spirit who indwells us is the Spirit of power.* Now I know that today, particularly, we think of the power of the Holy Spirit in terms of the extraordinary, gifts of the Spirit such as healing, tongues and even miracles that He may work through us or in us. But, in fact, that is not the biblical emphasis on the work of the Holy Spirit *at all.* The biblical teaching is that the power of the Spirit is more related to the lives of Christians than the extra gifts and signs. We are in danger of forgetting what the Holy Spirit has come to do. *He has come to enable us to live as the children of God, to empower us so that we might live to God's glory in the circumstances in which He has placed us.* What was the greatest work of the Holy Spirit? Supremely, we find that the work of the Holy Spirit was to raise Jesus Christ from the dead. It was through the power of the Holy Spirit that the actual dead body of the Lord Jesus was raised and transformed into His resurrection body which ascended to heaven. There is nothing greater than this. Fundamentally, we are dealing with this power of the Holy Spirit within the human body, this power which He has already exercised in you and me. When we were dead in trespasses and sins the great miracle was wrought in us so that we became alive unto God.

There is no greater miracle that will ever happen to us and all other miracles are small in comparison. The Lord Jesus said that when the Holy Spirit came his disciples would do greater works than He Himself did. The apostles never did greater miracles than our Lord so what were the 'greater works' that would be done through them? *It was the conversion of sinful men and women.* It is the power which brings them out of darkness into light, the power which changes the hearts of stone into hearts of flesh that respond to God. *This* is what has happened to us. Why are we interested in God? The answer is that God's Holy Spirit has changed us. The Bible says a new birth, a supernatural work, a new creation has taken place in us, and Paul said in his letter to the Philippians that this is the result of the power of the Holy Spirit in us.

What is more, in this natural world every man and woman is concerned with and governed by their senses. They live for and worship only what they can see, taste and touch, whereas the Christian is enabled to 'look not to the things that are seen but to the things that are unseen; for the things that are seen are transient, but the things that are unseen are eternal' (*2 Cor. 4:18*). This is what Stephen saw when he was being stoned to death so that he was able to say, 'Lord Jesus, receive my spirit . . . do not hold this sin against them' (*Acts 7:59–60*). It was these eternal things which so many martyrs saw and that is why they were willing to be put to death for their faith. Who is this person who has been able to transform fallen men and women so that they live for the unseen things of God, and so that the eternal things become more valuable to them than the things of time, even their own lives? This change has been wrought in us by the Spirit of God. Paul said that the Spirit of God has been given to us to change us, to transform us, to empower us to live the lives of the sons of God. He said, 'I can do all things in him.' We are in Christ through the work of the Holy Spirit in regeneration, through the work of the Holy Spirit who is empowering, enabling and quickening us. How does this take place? As the apostle wrote in Romans, it is the Holy Spirit who gives us the power to put to death the deeds of the body and who imparts to us a holiness which is not of our own making (*Rom. 8:13*). The fundamental work of the Holy Spirit is to enable us to live 'in Christ'.

This is what it means to be a Christian. We are the temples of the Holy Spirit and He is to enable us to live as the children of God in the situation in which He has placed us. So we must go back to God and say, 'You are my Father, You put me in this situation, You are calling on me to do things which I cannot do and bear things I cannot bear.' We must examine ourselves before God, ask ourselves what we are doing to quench the power of the Spirit within us; we must take our faith seriously. If Christ died for us in order to reconcile us to God then certain truths follow. This God who is our Father is for us, and He is the One who rules the universe and controls *all* the circumstances of our lives. He cares for us and therefore He will not afflict us without a loving purpose, neither will He test us above what we are able to bear. We are 'in Christ' so if God were ill-treating us He would be ill-treating His Son. We must go back on our knees and deal with God; instead of fighting His purposes we must genuinely seek His power to live to His glory even in the midst of our trials.

This is what it means to grow in faith and it means, moreover, that we are not looking to God only in the big things in life – forgiveness, eternal life, deliverance from hell and judgment, but we need to remind ourselves that God is also the God of the details. The Lord Jesus said that He clothes the grass, the birds of the air are fed by Him, and even the very hairs of our heads are numbered (*Matt. 6:26–30*). He *knows* the details. We say we believe the big things about God but we fail to believe Him in the small things.

So I want to remind you that when Paul said, 'I can do all things in him', he meant that he was in Christ, and that through the Holy Spirit the life of Christ was in him; he had learned the ways of God's grace to us through Christ. The art of living as Paul lived is by means of a *daily spiritual discipline*, using every means that God has given to us in order to let the power of Christ, through the Holy Spirit, flood our lives. Let us take God seriously, let us take the indwelling person of the Holy Spirit seriously, and you and I will learn to walk as Paul walked, as the children of God, with His peace and joy so that our lives glorify our Saviour. Sometimes we sing the hymn:

O Jesus Christ, grow Thou in me,
And all things else recede:
My heart be daily nearer Thee,
From sin be daily freed.

This is the *daily* consciousness that God Himself through His Spirit dwells in us that we might live to His glory in the place where He has put us. May God help us to live like this!

12 Practical Fellowship in Christ

I rejoice in the Lord greatly that now at length you have revived your concern for me; you were indeed concerned for me, but you had no opportunity . . . Yet it was kind of you to share my trouble. And you Philippians yourselves know that in the beginning of the gospel, when I left Macedonia, no church entered into partnership with me in giving and receiving except you only; for even in Thessalonica you sent me help once and again. Not that I seek the gift; but I seek the fruit which increases to your credit. I have received full payment, and more; I am filled, having received from Epaphroditus the gifts you sent, a fragrant offering, a sacrifice acceptable and pleasing to God.

Philippians 4:10, 14–18

One of the valuable things about systematic expository preaching is that you cover the same ground that the Bible covers. You not only preach the texts which appeal to you personally, but your subjects are governed by the text as you systematically go through each book or chapter. In this way you deal with every subject and every problem as it arises. I believe this is the right way to study the Scriptures because we discover more and more of what the New Testament tells us, that 'All Scripture is inspired by God and is profitable for teaching, for reproof, for correction and for training in righteousness, that the man of God may be complete, equipped for every good work' (*2 Tim. 3:16–17*). In other words, Christianity is concerned with life in all its fullness, and every aspect of it, and the Scriptures are to teach and guide us how to live in all kinds of situations, both individually and together as a community, as the church of God. Passages such as this one *ought* to be reckoned with as well as those more congenial to us. So may God help us as we look at a text which is of great practical importance, something, perhaps, about which we do not preach enough! But it affected the life of the apostle and it affects the life of each one of us in the church today.

THE DUTY OF THANKFULNESS

You will recall that I did not expound verse 10, but said that I would return to it when I reached verses 14–18 because really it is connected to these verses. Paul had received a gift from the Philippian church and the letter, as you know, was written partly to thank them for sending it: 'I rejoice in the Lord greatly that now at length you have revived your concern for me; you were indeed concerned for me, but you had no opportunity.' However, he knew that his words could have been misconstrued. He knew the opposition and, consequently, in case there was any misunderstanding or misapprehension, he continued by saying, 'Not that I complain of want; for I have learned in whatever state I am, to be content.' He said he had been through the school of Christ and he knew how to endure, how to live to the glory of God in all circumstances. He continued in verse 14 with 'Yet' – and the word is quite distinctive – 'it was kind of you to share my trouble'. It was right and proper for him to thank them although he knew that God was behind their action. They had not been obliged to send him this gift, it was something which they had organized; they had collected the money and sent it to Rome by the hand of Epaphroditus, and because Paul needed the help that they had sent him, he was grateful for it and so he thanked them.

This is the first lesson for us to learn. It is possible to be so independent in our spirits that we resent any gifts that are given to us even when we are in need. We can be so proud that we cannot really say 'thank you' and mean it. On the other hand, we can be so conceited that we take kindnesses for granted and do not even bother to show gratitude to people. But the fact is that none of us *is* independent; we all need one another, and we need one another in many different ways. Remember the analogy that the apostle used concerning the church. He referred to it as the body of Christ – one body because each member has been redeemed by Jesus Christ and is indwelt by the Holy Spirit. He likened the church to a human body which has different organs but each organ is dependent upon the others. For the proper function of the whole body all the different organs need to contribute and work together. Paul saw this as the function of the body of Christ, not only having spiritual fellowship together, but each part supporting the other according to its needs. In the light of this he thanked the Philippian church for the support they had given him.

At the same time, we can see that the apostle always looked beyond the actions of men and women; *he always saw God behind all the circumstances of his life* and so he began verse 10, 'I rejoice in the Lord greatly'. He thanked the Philippians for their gift but he still rejoiced *in the Lord* greatly because, he said, it was the Spirit of God who motivated them to do what they did. In other words, he retained his independence because he saw God overruling the actions of the Philippians and using them to meet his requirements. *His ultimate dependence was not on them but on God*. Moreover, he knew that he must not allow himself to be in a position where he was so dependent upon man that he could not retain his freedom to preach the gospel without respect to any person.

If he was sent a gift then he appreciated the kindness he had received, but above all he thanked God for it because, ultimately, he never saw himself as being dependent upon any man. Consequently you never find Paul asking for any help for himself; he asked others to organize help for the poor in Jerusalem; but he did not ask for anything for himself because he had to retain his dependence upon God for all his needs.

It was also important that Paul should retain his dignity. By this he did not mean the dignity of a sinful man, puffed up with pride in himself, although saved only by grace, but his dignity as a servant of Jesus Christ, before whom he stood. He wanted the Philippians to know that he was the servant of Christ and not the servant of any man or any church. Although he said, 'I rejoice in the Lord greatly that now at length you have revived your concern for me', he also said, 'Not that I complain of want', because God had taught him to depend utterly and completely upon Himself. He told them, 'I can do all things through Christ who strengthens me.' He thanked men but he thanked God too, and *in whatever situation he found himself his eyes were always upon God*. This is the right balance – we thank God for the works of men; we thank men for responding to the grace of God in them, but *it is God who is the prime mover in all the circumstances of our lives*.

PRACTICAL FELLOWSHIP

Verse 14 begins with, 'Yet it was kind of you to share my trouble'. Although the apostle was very much aware that God was at work in this gift he had received from the Philippians, yet he was grateful to them because they had responded to the movement of the Spirit of God within them and he acknowledged their kindness. He said, 'It was *kind* of you to share my trouble.' What did he mean? How could the Philippians, many miles away, share in his trouble? The

Greek word for 'trouble' means pressure – the troubles and afflictions that come from pressure. That is what he was referring to in this verse. What were these pressures? In the first place, as we have already seen, Paul was in prison; he was chained to Roman soldiers – and it does not take much imagination to guess what a Roman prison was like – and he was facing death. Also, wherever Paul travelled, whether he was in prison or not, he had to eat, and he needed clothes – these were his basic human needs. There were also the expenses of travelling, and he needed writing materials for his letters to the churches. He had to send his manuscripts to the churches but how could he do this unless there was money to pay for a messenger? These were the practical details of his life, his daily needs. Sometimes, it is true, Paul was able to work with his own hands. For instance, he stayed in Ephesus for some time and while there he was able to work, but this was not always possible because he was an itinerant preacher, he was a journeying missionary; and if he was to do the work to which God had called him he could not always work with his own hands. During these times he was utterly dependent upon God to supply his needs directly. But God does not manufacture gold coins in heaven, although some people seem to think He does! He does not print bank notes; they come from the church, they come from people, they come from individuals. It was the same in the days of Paul as it is today; he was dependent upon God moving the hearts of the Christians to be concerned for him.

Moreover, he told the Philippians that when they shared in the pressure of his needs as a human being they shared all the other pressures as well; they helped to relieve the pressure of the prison and the loneliness. Here were people who loved and cared for him *personally*. In verse 15 he said, 'You entered into partnership with me.' The Greek verbal root is – *koinōneō* – it means 'a partaker in' or 'a partaker with'; it is the root of the word 'fellowship'. He told them that they had fellowship with him in his troubles. This word fellowship is sometimes very misused these days. We spiritualize it to such an extent that it can mean only rather pious practices. We use the phrase 'talking about the Lord', which is right. Real fellowship *is* sharing with other Christians at a depth, sharing our spiritual experiences. But it also includes sharing their troubles, that is their loneliness, their burdens, and sometimes their financial needs. Sometimes it may involve sharing our homes, sharing our time by listening to those with troubles or visiting the ones who live alone, especially those who are housebound, giving out genuine, sometimes costly, Christian love where it is needed. True fellowship is not sharing in the things of God only on a doctrinal basis, although that is important, but it is sharing *with* people in practical terms when needed; *that is real fellowship*. Paul himself came down to very practical things – even money. So if you want to know what true fellowship is, this is the extent to which it goes, even as far as sharing our money! He reminded the Philippians in verse 15 that towards the beginning of his ministry when he left Macedonia, when they first received the gospel and the church was first formed, they had helped him. He told them, 'No church entered into partnership with me in giving and receiving except you only; for even in Thessalonica you sent me help once and again.' They entered into partnership with him when they undertook to help him financially both in giving and receiving – 'your expenditure, my receipt'. In other words, this church got together and decided to back Paul and support him in a practical way. In verse 16 he told them, not only 'once' you did it; they had helped him when he was in Thessalonica and now again when he was in Rome. They *looked* for opportunities to help him! He reminded them that they always had this concern for him but they had not had an opportunity to help him until now. They were a long way away; they had to gather a large sum of money together and pay for the expenses of Epaphroditus to cross the ocean in order to reach Rome so that the money could be given to him; there were no cheques and postal services in those days! This was *true* Christian fellowship. They thought of the apostle not only as a pastor but as a human being, just like any other human being who needed accommodation and food.

There are several lessons to be learned from this incident:

1. To be separated to God is not to be dehumanized. In other words, it does not mean that those who are separated to God cease to be human beings like everybody else, like other Christians. They have got the same needs, desires and hopes as everybody else. Nor does it mean that the church can be exempt from being realistic about these personal needs; as Christians we must be aware of these needs in a very practical way. This is what Paul meant when he told the Philippians, 'You shared my pressures.'

2. This special calling of God which separates people to Himself for ministerial service often brings greater temptations, greater attacks of the devil because these people become targets. There are pressures that people do not know anything about, but Paul knew about them. The devil will use every means, including money, health, sex, or any other means, to pull God's servants down, if he can stop them being instrumental in extending the kingdom of God and devoting themselves to the things of God as they seek to do.

3. Moreover, there are spiritual pressures, the responsibilities which come from being concerned in the spiritual welfare of a church and a community. As well as preaching, this involves many other things such as bringing before people the needs of others, whether the church itself, the unconverted, or those serving God abroad or in other parts of this country; planning for the future of the church, which sometimes includes large rebuilding programmes. Last, but not least, there is the pastoral care of any individuals who

need advice, support and encouragement with their various problems.

4. Add to these the persecution, opposition, and misunderstanding which came upon the apostle; he had no means of support and had to look to God entirely for his daily needs. He was telling the Philippians that they helped to lift part of his burden so that he was enabled to face the other burdens, which could not be shared. This is really what he meant. He knew that God, in His mercy, had put it into the hearts of these Philippians to share in the pressures of the work so that he was relieved where possible, and he thanks God for them. Paul was grateful that these people used their Christian common sense for the sake of the gospel, for the sake of the man whom God had separated to Himself in order to bring the gospel to them and build them up in the things of God. It is a sad fact that today many churches, many Christians, have not followed the example of the Philippians because they have relied upon the benefactors of the past generations and ignored their *personal* financial responsibilities towards the ministry.

SPIRITUAL ENCOURAGEMENT

'Not that I seek the gift; but I seek the fruit which increases to your credit.' The apostle in this verse told the Philippians that they had given to him abundantly; he was filled to overflowing and was grateful to them. But let us also note that in verse 17 he said, 'Not that I seek the gift; but I seek the fruit which increases to your credit.' Let us think for a moment why Paul said this. The difficulty was that the moment he indicated to people that he had needs, some of them charged him with being in the ministry because of what he could get out of it. On the other hand, if he had not said anything about his needs, he could have been accused of false humility. He was torn between the two.

But having shown these people that it was God for whom he lived, it was on God that he depended, he then looked at the spiritual encouragements of their gift.

1. *I seek the fruit*. The practical outworking of love towards God is concern for others, concern for the unconverted, and also concern for other Christians – the body of Christ. The sign of a healthy apple tree is fruit; this is what we expect in nature. If a tree does not give fruit in its season we ask what is wrong with it; we try to find out the reason for the lack of fruit; we are not content to let any time go by without doing something about it. In exactly the same way, the sign of the life of God in people is the love of God reaching out through them to the needs of others as it did through the Lord Jesus Christ. Paul had seen in these Philippians the fruit of the work of God. *This* was the sign, amongst others, that God was at work in their hearts and lives, and he was praising God for it. There is another point too; the Scriptures tell us that what we sow, we reap, and when people give to God I believe He blesses them, and this has been shown many times in the history of the church.

2. *A fragrant offering, a sacrifice acceptable and pleasing to God*. Paul called it a sacrifice, a sacrifice and a costly offering, a thank-offering to God. It was like the smoke of incense ascending to God, representing the worship of His people and giving joy to God. These were the words that he used about the gift of Christ Himself: 'Christ loved us and gave himself up for us, a fragrant offering and sacrifice to God' (*Eph. 5:2*). He knew that it had cost these Philippians to send this gift; it had meant a sacrifice in order to do it. But, you see, at the heart of Christianity there *is* a sacrifice – *the sacrifice of the cross of Jesus Christ*. There *is* a cross in all Christian commitment. But, he said, it is acceptable, it is well-pleasing to God. Their motives in giving to the apostle were right; they were concerned about him as a fellow Christian, they were concerned about the kingdom of God.

They gave because of gratitude for the gift of Jesus Christ; they gave because of their love to God. They were concerned about men and women receiving the good news of the gospel; they were concerned about this servant of God and, consequently, he says to them from God, 'Your gifts were a fragrant offering, a sacrifice acceptable and well-pleasing to God.' They did not give in order to make him feel indebted; they gave with the right motive. They were not like Cain, for whose gift God 'had no regard'.

What is the message for us behind these verses? It is that you and I claim to have received a gospel which is a gospel of grace, which is a gospel of *giving*. God *gave* His Son and God *gives* forgiveness freely; He *gives* us the righteousness of Christ freely so that we stand in His presence as Christ Himself stands. He gives us all these benefits not because we deserve them. By nature we are hell-deserving sinners. We have received the love of God to us in Christ as a *gift*. 'The wages of sin is death, but the free gift of God is eternal life in Christ Jesus our Lord' (*Rom. 6:23*). The unspeakable gift of God is Jesus Christ. Consequently, if we have received so much freely, the reality must be such that there must be within us an upsurge of love to God, a gratitude to God expressed in the fruit of our lives, each one of us seeking to further the gospel to all – near and far. We can help to provide the means whereby this glorious gospel should be proclaimed by God's messengers, separated to Himself, and thereby share with them in exalting Christ, and through Him, bring glory to God in this world. The Philippians did this by supporting those who were seeking to extend the kingdom of the Lord Jesus with its great message of love to the Roman world around them. May God help us to play our part in doing the same in our own day.

13
The Great and Glorious Supplier

My God will supply every need of yours according to his riches in glory in Christ Jesus. Philippians 4:19

I believe that when Paul wrote these words there was an element of rejoicing and perhaps even exuberance about them. You remember that he was chained in a Roman prison when he wrote to them, but despite his circumstances he *knew* that God was faithful and would be faithful to the Philippian church. If you recall the context, he was thanking the Philippians for having sent him what had obviously been a very large gift, which had abundantly satisfied his needs: 'I have received full payment, and more; I am filled, having received from Epaphroditus the gifts you sent' (*verse 18*). He was thrilled with what they had done. He told them that they had supplied his needs in an abundant way but, at the same time, he wanted them to know that God would supply any of their own needs which could have arisen as a result of their generosity to him. Indeed, he told them, God would supply *all* the needs in their lives, not just the financial ones: 'My God will supply *every* need of yours according to his riches in glory in Christ Jesus.' Is this true or is it only a platitude? Is this something we quote quite flippantly or is it part of our everyday experience? That is what really matters to us. Does God supply all our needs according to His riches in glory in

Christ Jesus? This text does not only mean our financial needs any more than it meant only the financial needs of the Philippians; it includes *all* our needs. This is a great promise; it is a great statement of assurance by the apostle and, in looking at it, we need to remind ourselves that God does not change; He is always the same. He is the same in our day as He was in the day of Paul and the Philippians, the same as when these words were spoken. Moreover, with God there are no favourites; he treats everybody according to the same principles, so this is a message of vital importance for us as well as for the Philippians. It is a challenge to us, particularly if our initial reaction to these words is: '*I* could not have written these words; this has not been my experience'. If God is the same and His power is the same it must be that the deficiency is in us. Perhaps we have been afraid to trust God or our faith has been so small that we have not trusted Him to supply the needs of which we have been so conscious. Maybe we have been reluctant to give financially because we wanted to guard ourselves, our futures, our own securities, and have spent too much of our energy and time on temporal things, so that we have forgotten God and acted as though He would not see what we had done. Then when needs have arisen we have even got out of the habit of looking to God to meet them. We have sought to satisfy them only by our own resources. God does not call anyone to act foolishly with money, but He does call upon us to live to Him first and foremost, to remember those in need, to support His work and care for those around us.

'*MY* GOD'

In this chapter we can see Paul in very different circumstances, under a sentence of death or the possibility of it, but in writing to these people he said, '*My* God'. There seemed to be almost a pride in his words. He did not say 'God' but '*My*

God'. He did not mean that God was his exclusive possession but that *God had become his personal God in life because He was the God whom he had experienced personally.* He was not talking about a philosophical thought or some unknown god whose altar he had seen in Athens some years before; he was talking about a God whom *he knew,* the One who had changed the course of his life, the One who had changed the quality of his life, the One who had changed the destiny of his life, the One who had changed the whole of his thinking about the world, about eternity, about everything in the world. He said, '*This God whom I have come to know – He is my God.*' I wonder if we can speak in these terms, because this is the great aim of Christianity – to bring us into a personal, living relationship with God through Jesus Christ and if it does not do that, then I do not know what else it does.

The second thing I would like to say about Paul's statement, '*My* God', is that he had this consciousness of God, if I may use the word, as a 'superb' God, somebody in whom he could glory. There was something wonderful about God, something which gave him joy even to think, to speak and to write about. He had known the faithfulness of God throughout the years. He had known the faithfulness of God towards him even when he had been unfaithful to God, so he knew that this God was not only a God of faithfulness but a God of mercy. It was God who had had the power to change him, to revolutionize him not only as an individual but to exercise this power through him towards others. He had known the detailed care of God in his life; time and time again the Spirit had led him, forbidding him to go into certain areas but telling him to go into others. There was the guidance, the directing – all that he had needed he had found in God. And, of course, he had found something else which was indescribable, he had found that this God loved him and had manifested His love to him in so many different ways. So he wrote, '*My* God', with this warmth of feeling; He is the God of creation and the God of providence over life but, above all, the God of grace, the God who had given him forgiveness freely, inexplicably, who had justified him and given him eternal life. No wonder he rejoiced in God!

Has God changed? Has Jesus Christ changed? I ask myself whether I am preaching as I ought to preach, that God forgives freely on account of the death of Jesus Christ; whether I am preaching that the most terrible sinner, anyone and everyone who is conscious of the weakness that is within him, never mind how deep that weakness is in his life, can come to God and, because of Jesus Christ, God freely forgives him. This is the grace of God, the unearned favour of God. Not only does God forgive the sinner but He restores him into His family and reckons him to be righteous in His sight day by day. Moreover, God tells us that He wants redeemed sinners to live with Him in His love, He wants them to live with Him eternally. It is because these eternal things have grown dim, these immense, unspeakable gifts of grace have lost their freshness, that we have turned our eyes to our temporal needs and they have become such pressing needs upon us; we look at them, we cherish them and we grieve over them, and it is these things that are taking up our minds.

We have lost this vision of the greatness, the immensity and the wonder of being forgiven by God, of being restored into His family, of belonging to Him, and of the glory waiting for us. The time will come when we will leave this world – it is only a matter of 60, 70, 80 years, or whatever it may be, but there is the whole of glory waiting for us for ever; we seem to lose the realization of this. Paul wrote these words in prison and what did he have outwardly, what possessions, what position, what wealth, what influence? As far as the world was concerned, here was a criminal awaiting trial; but this man had his eyes opened to heaven and to God. And he knew his God, he knew that this world was going to pass away; but God was waiting for him in glory; he would be absent from the body but present with the Lord which would be far better.

Can we say that our eyes are towards God and eternity as Paul's were? When we come to God for mercy we come empty-handed, but it is the knowledge of His love and grace for the world in Jesus Christ that is all-important. This is the foundation of all our growth in Him; it is the cross which is the foundation of everything else in our lives. It is the standard by which we look at everything else in life; God's love has been manifested in the cross. It is through His death that we will find eternal glory with Him. This is greater than all material blessings, for 'What will it profit a man, if he gains the whole world and loses his own soul?' (*Matt. 16:26*). That is the value that our Lord put upon eternal life. So when Paul spoke to the Philippian church about God he said, '*My* God'. I wonder how many of us think of God in this way and, if we do not, is it because we have allowed temporal needs to dominate us? Have we lost sight of the great things that He has done for us in Jesus Christ? *These are the eternal things, the unchangeable things*, the things of glory and the kingdom of God, and all that it means to be a member of that kingdom.

'YOUR NEEDS'

But, he went on to say, 'My God will supply all your needs. This was a great claim, and let us not run away from it but consider a few things about it. Although he said, 'My God will supply all your needs', that does not mean our luxuries or our optional extras but it means our essential requirements. In an affluent society it is easy to think that our luxuries are our needs! Putting it in another way, Paul was telling the Philippians that whatever they lacked as a result of their gift to him God would repay them so that they could live to His glory. But it was not only the Philippians who had needs. If we talked to one another freely we would find that we *all* have needs. First there are the role needs – as father, mother, businessman, scholar, housewife, teacher, pastor. Whatever it is that we are doing we have responsibilities attached to that role, we have pressure points, we have needs in that particular sphere, and we have to live in these roles to the glory of God. Then we have all got temporal needs in one way or another, circumstances that we want to change, economic pressures, job prospects, unemployment, the question of marriage and other relationships, even finding accommodation, and many other everyday needs. They are needs which involve us in problems of one kind or another. There are also our physical needs, lack of good health, especially as we grow older, the pains and aches which come upon us, being house-bound, loneliness which is so often permanent, the fear of death, the nearness of death, all these needs seem to be daily with us. Lastly, there are what I call spiritual needs – overcoming sin, growing into the likeness of the Lord Jesus Christ, resisting temptations, having the courage to be Christians where we are, where God has put us, without complaining and grumbling, enduring afflictions, facing death in the Lord Jesus Christ with the glory of heaven before us, and having the peace that passes all understanding. All these things are needs, and Paul's message to these people was, 'My God will supply *all* your needs.'

Let me make a few observations about this. It is not a promise that we shall be exempt from or even delivered out of afflictions. After all Paul wrote this while being held captive in a Roman prison and God had not delivered him thus far! In this instance, God's purpose was to deliver him and he was released for a short time, but later on when he returned to prison he was executed. So do not let us get the idea that what this promises is freedom from afflictions or freedom from death. It does not promise this. What is Paul saying then? He is saying that *God in His mercy will provide all that we need, the inner strength, the comfort and power to live to the glory of God in the circumstances in which He has placed us*. It is clear from the Scriptures that sometimes deliverance from affliction *is* God's provision as when He delivered Peter from prison in a miraculous way (*Acts 12:7*). At other times He allows us to suffer like James who was slain by the sword (*Acts 12:2*), and as, indeed, Paul himself was executed. However, I believe that God *does* repay our sacrifices, that what we sow we reap, not only in eternity but in this life also. Sometimes we can see this proved in a very practical way. Our Lord told the disciples, 'Truly, I say to you, there is no man who has left house or wife or brothers or parents or children, for the sake of the kingdom of God, who will not receive manifold more in this time, and in the age to come eternal life' (*Luke 18:29–30*). Paul was saying that if we sow to God financially as these Philippians had done, He would not be unmindful, He would repay. There are many Christians who have proved that giving to God has been rather like an investment and instead of any lack they have found that God has given back to them financially. It was not that they gave for that purpose, because that would have been a very wrong motive, but God has indeed prospered them.

HIS RESOURCES

Moreover, God *does* give the inner strength, comfort and power to live in and through the circumstances He allows, and *the Christian life is a challenge to experience the resources of God in our own particular circumstances, however difficult they may be*. But the only way we will find these resources is by relating our lives to God, relating them to God in prayer, telling Him about our problems, and continually asking Him for help and strength. When we pray we must use the many promises He has given us in His Word, promises given to us for encouragement, strength and assurance. When we come to God in prayer we must remind ourselves of these promises and quote them in our prayers. This is why it is so important for us to study and know the Word of God, know how He dealt with His people through the ages; this is our foundation. Then we must live out in practice the indwelling of the Holy Spirit, who has been given to each one of us at our new birth. This does not mean that by our own supreme efforts, by sheer will power, by stoicism, we attain success. Because it is only by the grace of the Holy Spirit who indwells us that we are able to apply these promises to our own lives and find the resources of God through them. Here was a man who had been shipwrecked, beaten, half-starved, who had suffered all kinds of conditions and experienced many problems, but in the end he said, '*I have found that God is able to give me what is necessary to live to His glory.*' This man challenges us all. When our needs are not met I do not believe the fault is in God; the fault lies in us that we are not going back to God to take hold of the resources that are available to us through the Holy Spirit. God's promises are the same promises to us today as they were to Paul. Whatever our needs are He will give us those things, whether it is money, accommodation, guidance concerning our future, guidance in business, strength, comfort; whatever our needs are He will supply them. The apostle was telling these Philippians, and us, that even if they were in prison they would find grace to live there to the glory of God; if they were under sentence of death or the possibility of it they would find that they would be able to rejoice in the Lord always, as he was rejoicing. *This was his experience of God.*

Paul was very clear about these things. He said, 'My God will supply every need of yours according to his riches in glory.' In other words, in glory there are riches of God that He can give to His people according to His will; *they are unlimited and He gives bountifully; He is a generous God.* This is the thought behind what Paul was writing. Is this true? Do we live as though we are in the presence of a God who is unlimited? At times I find it very difficult, sometimes I find that my faith is not what it ought to be, but the fault is in me and not in God. It may be that we need to go back to God and repent of our unbelief in His presence because He has given us so many great examples of His faithfulness. Remember how He delivered the children of Israel from Pharaoh at the Red Sea, how He supplied their needs during their journey in the wilderness and finally brought them into the promised land. Then, years later, when God wanted to move His people from Babylon He raised up a man called Cyrus to be king of Persia. He inspired him to deliver the Jewish people from exile in Babylon, and he was responsible for the rebuilding of the temple in Jerusalem. Cyrus was the means whereby God fulfilled His plan for His chosen people. When God wants to break into a situation, His forces, His powers are unlimited. When God wants to act there is no man who can stop Him, and let us not forget that *God is still the same today; He has the same resources*.

Much nearer to our own time there have been people who have found this, people like George Müller who founded a very large orphanage in Bristol simply by trusting in God to meet the daily needs of hundreds of orphan children. What about Hudson Taylor, who founded the China Inland Mission and trusted God to provide the means to enable so many missionaries to take the gospel into China? These men *proved* that God does supply our needs if we really trust Him. He has unlimited ways and means to meet our needs. The Bible teaches us that this is also true when it comes to giving us strength, giving us comfort; He *will* provide. 'Likewise the Spirit helps us in our weakness' (*Rom. 8:26*). He is the 'God of all comfort, who comforteth us in all our tribulations' (*2 Cor. 1:3–4*). When we come to church, I wonder whether we come with an expectation that God will meet us, to encourage, to strengthen us, to meet our needs spiritually so that when we use the means that He has given us – the Bible, the sermon, the Communion Service, the prayers, the worship, the Christian fellowship – God through His Holy Spirit can give us what we need from His unlimited resources. We may feel sometimes that we can believe that God will supply the needs which other people have, but it is harder for us to believe that He can supply our own particular needs; our own needs seem more difficult than those of other people! But Paul says here, 'My God will supply *every need of yours*.' If we do not find these resources at first then we must go back to him until He does meet us; we must be like the importunate widow who persisted in her request until she was vindicated (*Luke 18:2–5*).

It is also true that there is a providential ordering of life, and God is able to order things in ways which are beyond our understanding. Take the example of Joseph who was taken down into Egypt as a slave. God had chosen this young man to be prime minister of Egypt, which was the greatest power on earth in those days. We all know the story well. He was brought from prison to a place of great authority in order to save his own nation in a time of famine. Then there was the timing of David's visit to his brothers, who had gone to battle against the Philistines. David was sent by his father to take them food. He was there on the battlefield at just the right time to hear Goliath's challenge, and he became the instrument in God's hands to deliver Israel from Goliath and the Philistines, and ultimately this led him to the throne of Israel. We have another example when we see how the ancient world was prepared for the gospel. There was a stable government under the Roman emperor Caesar; communications were better in those days than for many years to come; there was a common language; many synagogues had been built in the land; and it seems that Christianity came when everything was ready for a rapid spread of the gospel. God was working through nations, providentially ordering all these things in order to fulfil His purpose of spreading the gospel of Jesus Christ not only to the Jews but also to the Gentiles. God was able to bring about His purposes in a heathen world and He can do it in our day and age too. This is what I mean by the unlimited resources of God; this is how God demonstrates to us His unlimited power to fulfil His purpose. He has a purpose for you, He has a purpose for me, and *He has a purpose for every Christian.* He wants every Christian to live to His glory and He is no respecter of persons. Do not ever let the devil tell you that you are too ordinary, too weak, too old, or even too ill for God to have a purpose for your life. That is a complete lie and a direct contradiction of God's Word to us. The devil wants us to believe these lies about ourselves because they are the very things that will prevent us living our lives to the glory of God. Now I know that sometimes these things are hard to accept, especially when we have to wait for God, but we must go back to Him and still wait and still argue in His presence and plead with Him because God *does* listen to us. It is the Holy Spirit who puts the urge in our hearts to cry to God to meet our needs. Let us follow that urge.

Paul talked about the 'riches in glory', the glorious resources of God to fulfil His purposes and to satisfy our needs – *all our needs.* The trouble with us is that, so often, we do not trust Him because we forget who He is and we need to be reminded of this; we need to be reminded of His resources. Let us remember that the extent of God's giving to us is to be measured in the gift of His Son. When you are up against things in life, when all the difficulties are before your eyes and deliverance seems impossible, remind yourself of the greatness of God's gift in His Son; if 'He . . . spared not his own Son but freely offered him up for us all, how shall he not with him also freely give us all things?' (*Rom. 8:32*). The bountiful giving of God must be measured by these gifts of grace; go back to Him and see Him afresh, ask Him to reveal Himself to you afresh. Let us remember that *God is not a reluctant giver; it is we who are reluctant receivers*. Not only has He forgiven us freely but He has imputed His own righteousness to us, He has reconciled us into His family and made us joint-heirs with Jesus Christ. He saves us through His Son and sanctifies us through His Holy Spirit. All these gifts are the measureless bounty of God towards us. It is through these eternal *facts* that Paul saw God, so he knew that this God would supply all the temporal needs of the Philippians.

'IN CHRIST JESUS' – HIS AGENT

Finally, Paul says, 'My God will supply every need of yours according to his riches in glory *in Christ Jesus*.' We as Christians may say, 'Ah, but I am not a very good Christian, I feel I am not as obedient as I ought to be. Yes, I have received the Lord Jesus but there is the weakness of the flesh. I am weak in faith, I fail in obedience. How can God ever meet my needs?' Paul said that God's goodwill is not dependent upon our merits, not even upon our efforts to believe and to be obedient, but only on the grounds of the person of Jesus Christ. *All our needs are met in Him*. He is the Mediator and Intercessor; it is because of His atoning death that we have forgiveness in His blood; we are at peace with God through the cross of Jesus Christ. God treats you and me as His sons and daughters *because we are in Christ.* We are made righteous through His obedience, made holy by His Spirit, we have eternal life through His giving. It is because of the cross of Jesus Christ that God is free to work on our behalf; through Him we have been reconciled to God, through Jesus Christ He prepares us to be the bride of His Son. Through Jesus Christ God is 'for' us and 'if God be for us who can be against us?' These are the unchangeable facts and they do not depend on our changeable feelings or circumstances.

Paul ends this practical message by focusing attention on the person of the Saviour; he calls the Philippians to wonder and glory in Jesus Christ, and I call on you to do the same. To those of you who are apart from Christ, what do you lack? Seek it in Christ, whether it be repentance or faith. I leave you with this wonderful passage, this wonderful promise, this great confidence. Let all of us, with all our needs, renew our faith in the resources of God. This is what it means for us to live as the children of God in our difficult circumstances in this world. If through Christ these *eternal* things have been effected, how much more ought we to trust God for the temporal things of life. We can look to God to provide all that we need of His riches in glory in Jesus Christ. God give us grace to prove the truth of these words in our own lives, in our own situation, in our own age.

14
To God Be the Glory

To our God and Father be glory for ever and ever. Amen.
Philippians 4:20

Verse 20 is really the closing verse of this remarkable letter of Paul to the Philippian church. Although two more verses follow, this is the end of the letter as such that is, the end of the *substance* of the letter. In it we discover a note of adoration, worship, and praise. Even in just reading it – 'To our God and Father be glory for ever and ever. Amen' – you surely catch something of the feelings as well as the thoughts of the apostle as he concluded this letter to the Philippians. And, of course, it is a good thing to remind ourselves that true and genuine Christian experience does not leave us unmoved emotionally. Christianity is not an intellectual exercise which merely satisfies the reason in some cold and academic manner; it is a way of life which embraces the whole personality; it steels the will and moves the heart to worship, to adoration and to praise. *After all, the very essence of the gospel itself is to bring man, as a whole being, back to God*; and here we find a hint of the God to whom we have been brought. It draws from Paul this cry of adoration, 'To our God and Father be glory for ever and ever. Amen.'

It is a good question to ask ourselves when we last uttered anything like this when praying on our own. I know we do so in church. In liturgical worship we say, 'Glory be to the Father and to the Son and to the Holy Spirit. As it was in the beginning is now, and ever shall be, world without end. Amen.' Probably we have said this thousands of times, but I wonder if we have ever said it *alone*. We may look back and say, 'Well, as a matter of fact, I remember times when I *have* felt the nearness of God, when I have worshipped Him. There have been times when He has given me a particular answer to prayer, a token of His love and mercy, some special guidance or uplift in one way or another, some tangible gift of grace, so to speak. I have been very thankful to Him then.' Good, that is how it should be! But that is not all. Here is, it seems to me, something greater and deeper. Here is the apostle, this amazing man, yet a man of like passions as we are, who, at the time he wrote this, was locked up in a dark prison, cut off from his great love of proclaiming the gospel of the Lord Jesus Christ and facing execution. Yet, having reminded the Philippians of their graciousness to him and of God's great ability not only to supply his own needs but their needs also, he goes on to say, 'To our God and Father be glory for ever and ever. Amen.' Now I wonder how often you and I, in the quietness of our own homes, have knelt in the presence of God and said to Him, 'Glory be to You, Father, Son and Holy Spirit'? And if we have not done this, why have we not done it? Is not our God worthy to be praised? As you know, in this letter, time and time again, Paul has urged upon us to rejoice in the Lord – 'Yes, and I shall rejoice' (*1:19*); 'Likewise you also should be glad and rejoice with me' (*2:18*); 'Finally, my brethren, rejoice in the Lord' (*3:1*); 'Rejoice in the Lord always; again I will say, Rejoice' (*4:4*). So it is fitting that he should end this letter on a note of praise and adoration. But how does he do it? That is what I am going to deal with in the rest of this sermon.

In a nutshell, the trouble with us is that we become so caught up with our immediate circumstances that we do not stand back and look at the eternal realities in which we are involved. As we have already seen, it is the *immediate* problems and difficulties that occupy our hearts and minds so much. It is right and proper that we *should* be concerned about these things, but not so concerned that we neglect to do what Paul did here when he lifted his eyes from the prison and even from the needs of the Philippian church. He lifted them up to God and he began to look at God in all His glory, in His eternity; he looked at the great purposes of God in which he himself was involved and his heart burst into praise as he said, 'Glory be to God, our Father.' This is what is wrong with us so often – *we do not lift our eyes up to God, to the eternal God.*

'TO OUR GOD AND FATHER'

Let us consider for a moment the phrase 'to our *God*'. Remember that the Philippian church was surrounded by many gods, scores of gods; it was a world peopled with semi-human divinities. But it was not these gods to which he was referring but to God the Father, the God-man Jesus Christ and God the Holy Spirit – to *our* God. He was thinking of God the Creator, the sovereign Lord of the universe, the only eternal and unchangeable God, the holy and righteous God who, despite His holiness and majesty, is merciful to sinners, to men and women. He was remembering the God of love, the supreme Being from whom everything comes and for whom all things exist, whose eternal purposes are being worked out in the history of mankind, and the apostle *knew* he was part of this plan. He said, '*This* is our God.' Our God is 'the Father of lights with whom there is no variation or shadow due to change' (*James 1:17*). He was reminding the Philippians that *this* was the eternal and everlasting God, not those fickle, phoney gods of Greece and Rome. He was not any neutral force which was permeating this universe, not even the unknown god of the altar in Athens. No, this was the God who had revealed Himself in creation and supremely in Jesus Christ our Lord, almighty and all-glorious, and yet a God of redemption and love. But do we ever think of God like this? Do we ever dwell upon the greatness and glory of God? Do we ever get on our knees and say to God, 'I thank You for what You are in Yourself'?

But there is another aspect of this whole situation. *Paul cannot think of God without thinking of the relationship into which he had been brought with Him.* He had been brought into a position where he could say 'our God and *Father*' – he had a relationship with God. This mighty and eternal Being who had created everything was, at the same time, the One with whom he had the relationship of a son to a father. God had deigned to give a sinful, mortal human being the right to call Him Father, and He has used this very close bond of fatherhood to convey His love towards us. The Lord Jesus said, 'Pray then like this, "*Our Father* who art in Heaven"' (*Matt. 6:9*). Despite all the teaching that there was at that time, the philosophies, the confusion of thought concerning all the gods – and they have got to be read about to be believed because they were so fantastic – the apostle said, '*God is a Father.*'

We can *know* that God is our Father, with all that that word means, and we can know the comfort that it brings to us in our own lives. We know the love and concern of our own earthly fathers. God has told us that He wants us to think of Him as our heavenly Father, and that we can live out this earthly pilgrimage in the light of the love of God to us as our Father with all the graciousness and joyfulness of this relationship.

But there is more to be seen in this relationship – *it is an eternal relationship.* In other words, it is a permanent relationship. When Paul was in prison things were rough for a while, with a death sentence hanging over him and not knowing what the outcome would be. He was chained and confined and we do not know what he was suffering; he was an old man whose body had been affected by his sufferings as a soldier of Jesus Christ. But one thing did not change and had never changed: he was still a son of God, he would always be a son of God, and when he died he would go to live eternally in the presence of God. *His circumstances had changed but his eternal relationship to God would never change.* This was greater than anything this world could ever bring against him. He knew that even if they executed him he would go home to be with his Father. Is this not true of us too? Stand back sometimes, lose these immediate, present things, stand back and see the perfection of what God has done for you and the grace of God in this relationship which is made perfect through Jesus Christ. We do not attain it by good works and sacrifices; God places us in this eternal relationship to Himself as a free gift because of the death of His Son on our behalf. There is nothing half-hearted about His gift to us; we stand in His presence now, clothed with the righteousness of Jesus Christ, and God treats us as His children.

What is more, the apostle had found a transforming power. He found, in fact, that the power of God had taken hold of him so that although he was living in this world with all its trials, what was real to him were the eternal things. Here is the man who wrote, 'We look not at the things which are seen but at the things which are not seen: for the things which are seen are temporal; but the things which are not seen are eternal' (*2 Cor. 4:18*). This was the great fundamental change: he had seen what cannot be seen with human eyes; he had seen the spiritual things, the things of God, the things of eternity, and more and more his life had been conformed to the life of God by the power of God's Spirit within him. Are these things not true about us too? Have we not begun in these things? The guilt of sin which troubled so many of us has been removed in Jesus Christ; the blood of Jesus Christ, God's Son, cleanses us from all sin. We have a permanent access into the presence of God as Father because we have been accepted as righteous in His sight. The very life that we live on earth has been transformed from a meaningless repetition of details and circumstances which end in a nothingness, into a pilgrimage whereby we *know* that we are journeying to our home, to our heavenly home, to be with our Father; *this* is the vision that is in front of us. It is like Bunyan's pilgrim's progress to the holy city where the multitude of the redeemed cry, 'Hallelujah, glory be to God on high'. These were the thoughts about God that passed through Paul's mind in prison, as we know from his epistles, and my prayer is that we too will stand back more often and look at these great things that God has done for us in Jesus Christ.

GLORY BE TO GOD

What does it mean when he says, 'To our God and Father be glory'? Putting it in a different way, it is the same as saying, 'Honour be to God'. Give God His rightful praise, extol His gloriousness. Worship and adore Him for His mercy and grace. Set out His love and grace, His mercy and longsuffering so that all can *behold* the majesty of His person and His faithfulness to man. Are not these glorious attributes true? Why is it that we do not praise and worship Him more often?

When God created our first parents they were created in the image of God with all the righteousness of created beings, not the righteousness which came about from their own efforts. But God gives us – imputes is the word we use – the divine righteousness of Jesus Christ which brings us to God and to heaven. As one great Puritan writer put it: 'In redemption is greater love, greater mercy and greater goodness than was given to Adam in innocency' (R. Sibbes). Adam was in a state of probation, dependent upon his own works, whereas we are 'accepted in the beloved', we live in a state of grace, heirs of glory and eternal life. We are to be as the bride of Christ. Think of the glory of God in reconciling justice and mercy! Justice was met in the body of Jesus Christ on the cross, mercy was the putting of our sins upon Him as our substitute and giving us His righteousness. We are forgiven, restored, accepted, and reconciled to God in Jesus Christ. So the heart of the matter lies in the goodness and grace of God towards us which passes understanding. Let us lose sight at times of the immediate things that are pressing upon us and let us return to these eternal things which are also true of us. What is more, they are unchangeably true of us, whether it be in life or in death.

Then there is the glory of God in Jesus Christ who, with all the perfection of the presence of His Father, came down to be born as a human being, to live in this world with all its tensions, its problems and its sin, and finally to end His life like a criminal hung upon a cross by the hands of His own people. But He rose again and He is still interceding for us, our ever-living High Priest. Moreover, He has promised not only to save us but to keep us and to continue this work in us to the end of our lives, and He has done all this for us because He loves us. Our bodies are to be the temples of the Holy Spirit; He has come to dwell in these wretched bodies of ours, and it is He who works righteousness in us and sheds the love of God abroad in our hearts. Do you wonder that this man in his prison lifted his eyes from his surroundings and lifted them to heaven saying: 'To our God and Father be glory for ever and ever'? Do not live in particular events only – stand back and take a panoramic view of God's glorious work, His plan of redemption for man.

'FOR EVER AND EVER'

Why did he say this? Because, as I have already been saying, these are not temporal things, they are not passing whims or the philosophies of the times; these are the eternal things, the unchangeable things, the irreversible truths about God, therefore they can be ascribed to Him for ever and ever. *These truths are the very foundation of our faith, from which we look at all the circumstances which beset us in life*. We read that in heaven itself the song continues. What is the eternal song? 'After this I heard what seemed to be the mighty voice of a great multitude in heaven, crying, "Hallelujah! Salvation and glory and power belong to our God . . . Hallelujah! For the Lord our God the Almighty reigns. Let us rejoice and exult and give him the glory, for the marriage of the Lamb has come, and his Bride has made herself ready"' (*Rev. 19:1, 6–7*). This is why the apostle was able to rejoice in God in such adverse circumstances, with such a bleak future in front of him. *These truths are eternal*; they are about God, and He is faithful to His promises. So Paul says, 'To our God and Father be glory for ever and ever.'

'AMEN'

And then he adds this word 'Amen'. It was a godly old Puritan called Thomas Adams who reminded us that this word 'Amen' has four meanings, and I mention them to you briefly here. When we say 'Amen' we say, 'So let it be'. It is a *confirmation* of our hearts' desires. When we hear the prayers of others we say 'Amen'; we confirm that it is our hearts' desire that God should answer these prayers. We say, 'Amen' because we approve of what is being prayed; it is a verbal sign that in spirit we are behind the prayers which are offered. Secondly, 'Amen' is also an *affirmation of our faith* because we never say 'Amen' to what we do not believe – at least I hope we do not! When I say, 'Glory to God our Father for ever and ever', can you really say, 'Amen, so let it be: I want to give glory to God; it is my heart's desire'? If indeed you do not believe in the Lord Jesus Christ you cannot say, 'Amen'; you cannot confirm that this is your heart's desire, that you love the Lord Jesus Christ, that you want to exalt God the Father, God the Son, and God the Holy Spirit. You cannot say 'Amen' to these truths.

There is a third meaning and it is an *acclamation*. In the Old Testament the word 'Amen' is used on the occasion of the anointing of a king, when he was brought out by the prophets of God. The prophet said, 'God save the King', and all the people said, 'Amen'. It was an acclamation that they received him as their king. Can you claim Him as your king? Oh, that in your hearts you can get down before Him and say to Him, 'Amen, You are *my* King. Glory be to You, my Father, to You, the Lord Jesus my Saviour, to You, Holy Spirit, who comes to dwell within me. I want to exalt You as God, the sovereign Ruler of my life. I want to say, "Amen" to You.' And finally, 'Amen' is seen as a *resolution*, as though we are pledging ourselves to say, 'I will resolve to glorify God in my life', which is a very solemn thing to say. It means resolving to glorify God all day and every day for the rest of our lives. Here is the apostle in this prison, looking to God, calling upon the Philippians to join him. He says 'To our God and Father be glory for ever and ever. Amen.' He is calling upon us to join with him too. My prayer is that you and I can say, 'Amen' to this verse.

15
The Grace of the Lord Jesus Christ

Greet every saint in Christ Jesus. The brethren who are with me greet you. All the saints greet you, especially those of Caesar's household. The grace of the Lord Jesus Christ be with your spirit.
Philippians 4:21–3

In his letters Paul always began with an introduction and ended with some form of greeting and a more personal note. So this great and wonderful letter of the apostle Paul to the Philippians comes to its close with greetings from those in Rome who had stood by him. His heart had been full of worship – you remember verse 20: 'To our God and Father be glory for ever and ever. Amen.' So there was nothing more to say except to end his letter by sending these personal greetings.

Before we get down to the main part of the sermon I am rather interested as to what was in the mind of Paul when he said, 'Greet every saint in Christ Jesus'. His heart was overflowing with love and the consciousness of what God has done for us as Christians, for every one of us who names the name of Christ is beloved of God, redeemed by the Lord Jesus Christ and indwelt by the Holy Spirit. There is a deep and fundamental unity among all who are Christians, which neither race, age, denomination, class, time, nor distance can in any way blur, and it is the tragedy of the Christian church that we have allowed secondary things to come between us when, in fact, we are all one in Christ Jesus.

It seems to me that in this verse there was a special word for the Christians at Philippi from the saints of Caesar's household. We are not quite sure of the identity of these people, but probably they were slaves and servants who worked in the imperial palace. I admit I am speculating, but I wonder if they were specially mentioned because they had been touched by the love and care of the Philippian church for the aged apostle in his tribulations and imprisonment. So when Paul was sending Epaphroditus back to Philippi with this letter, they wanted to be associated with him in sending greetings to this remarkable church who had cared about their minister, this man of God, the apostle Paul. I pass it on for your consideration.

We come to this final sentence: 'The grace of the Lord Jesus Christ be with your spirit.' These words refer, as one writer put it, to the 'inner personality, viewed as the contact point between God and His child'. Paul is ever mindful that fundamentally we should be concerned with the realm of the spirit, which matters above everything else in this world and in the world to come, the relationship between God and man, the realm where grace is operative. What did Paul mean when he used these words, and why did he want the grace of the Lord Jesus Christ to be with them? I think the best way for us to look at this is to go back, if you like, into the heart of the apostle Paul, to that experience from which everything else in his life flowed, the place where he first experienced the grace of the Lord Jesus Christ.

A CONVERSION TO GRACE

Before his conversion Paul was a dyed-in-the-wool Jew. He believed passionately in God, the God of Israel, who had revealed and covenanted Himself in a special way to His people. He believed that obedience to the Jewish law, and the traditions which had grown from it, was essential in order to be right with God, and he set about living in such a way that he was one of the foremost men in his generation in following the ways of the law and of God. Indeed, his zeal for his religion was such that when certain Jews spoke of Jesus as the Messiah, the Saviour, it was his mistaken zeal which caused him to persecute them, to attack them as deceivers and Jesus as the arch-deceiver. So he set out to destroy them, to have them incarcerated in prisons and, indeed, to have Stephen murdered. I am concerned with the way in which God dealt with Paul because it is the way in which in principle, or in method if you like, He deals with every one of us. I want to explain what he meant by the grace of the Lord Jesus Christ, because without it we will find that we are nothing in the sight of God. So let us examine this experience of Paul.

Here was this zealous Jew, persecuting the Lord Jesus Christ and His followers because they claimed that He was God incarnate, that God had come into this world in the person of Jesus Christ and was born of the Virgin Mary by the work of the Holy Spirit. Although He was divine He took upon Himself human life. He was judged, condemned and died, crucified upon a cross in disgrace, bringing upon Himself the curse of the law. It was *this* man whom His followers claimed to be the Messiah, the King who was to redeem the nation. To Paul it was blasphemous; they were destroying the Hope of Israel, the Messiah, the priestly King and Conqueror.

Moreover, these people claimed that they were right with God because they believed in this Jesus, not because they were members of the covenant, who had been circumcised and who kept the law. They were striking at the very root of his religion which meant living according to God's law in order to please Him and remain in His favour. If these people were right he was fundamentally wrong, but he believed he *was* right; the law was on his side, so this Man's teaching and all His followers must be exterminated.

What is more, they claimed that this Jesus was divinely alive while Paul *knew* that He had been crucified. They were not only deceived but they were beginning to propagate this belief in the resurrection, undermining the whole of the religion of the day. They were subverters of Judaism, enemies of the faith of Israel, so they had to be exterminated; and he was on the road to Damascus with this very purpose in mind.

Now I have built up this picture from the facts that we read about Saul of Tarsus, as he was known then. He hated Jesus and all that He represented and the people who followed Him. But on the road to Damascus Saul the persecutor was confronted with the person of Jesus Christ the risen Saviour, and consequently, once and for ever, certain issues were settled in his mind and settled without doubt. *Jesus was alive*! He spoke to Paul – person to person – and the first thing that Paul did when he went into Damascus was to prove that Jesus was the Son of God (*Acts 9:22*). Moreover, he preached that not only was this Jesus alive but *He was gloriously alive*. It was not some disembodied spirit or ghoul that he had seen; he had been confronted with the glory of the risen Christ in all His splendour, with the brightness which was above that of the midday sun, someone majestic who had the stamp of divinity. So he fell down at the feet of Christ the Lord because he knew that he was in the presence of God. Indeed, Jesus was not only gloriously alive but *He was divinely alive*, if I may put it that way. He knew exactly where the apostle was on the road to Damascus; He knew his innermost thoughts, his difficulties and problems, the hidden pricks of conscience that were in his mind, and He said to him: 'Saul, Saul, why are you persecuting me? . . . I am Jesus, whom you are persecuting: it is hard for you to kick against the pricks; but rise and enter the city, and you will be told what you are to do' (*Acts 9:4–6*). *From the beginning the Lord Jesus dealt with him fundamentally as God*; He changed this man Saul to become Paul the servant, the slave, the missionary, the man who gave Him obedience throughout his life until in the end he gave his life for the Lord Jesus. The object of his worship and obedience was the Lord; his submission was total – '*Lord*, what wilt thou have me to do?'

There are two points which this text makes clear – it declares the *divinity* of the Lord Jesus Christ and also the *grace* of the Lord Jesus Christ. I mention this particularly because a book has been published recently by some Anglican scholars and in it there are two avenues of thought which are very subtle. Firstly, the writers are trying to express the uniqueness of Christ in a way which is acceptable to people in these present days, so they try to find alternative words for the incarnation and the Son of God, but in doing this they fail to guard the divinity of the Lord Jesus Christ. In fact, there are various statements which imply that they decry Him. They give Him a unique place, but it is the *divinity of the Lord Jesus* which is questioned and challenged.

First of all, let us look at Paul's experience more carefully. These theologians believe that this experience of Paul *did* take place, but they think that there was perhaps a psychological reason for what happened to him. If they are right, then Paul was fundamentally wrong; Jesus is *not* the Son of God and Paul could not have met Him on this road to Damascus in the way that the Acts of the Apostles tells us. He was deceived, his glorious missionary life was based on self-deception, the thousands of people converted by his labours, and the millions by his writings, have all been deceived. I confess that I find it amazing that men of intelligence could think that after nineteen hundred years they know better than the person who was actually involved in this experience! After nineteen hundred years they believe they have suddenly discovered the truth which has been hidden from the church for all this time! On the other hand, it is not surprising that they have come to this conclusion because they have only reached the place from which they started! They do not believe that God breaks into human life; they do not believe in the miracles of the Lord Jesus Christ, the virgin birth, or the resurrection. In other words, they start reading the New Testament, having already decided that they are going to cut out the miraculous. But if they are going to press this to its logical conclusion, they must do away with the divinity of our Lord. They have approached this with their own philosophy and set themselves up as their own gods instead of submitting to the revelation of God Himself; *they* have decided what is to be the revelation of God, which is a very serious thing indeed.

Paul realized that the resurrection was crucial and that his independent experience confirmed and corroborated the evidence of the apostles. There were diverse theories about it even then but he answered them by giving the *facts*: 'that he was buried, that he was raised on the third day in accordance with the scriptures, and that he appeared to Cephas, then to the twelve. Then he appeared to more than five hundred brethren at one time, most of whom are still alive, though some have fallen asleep. Then he appeared to James, then to all the apostles. Last of all, as to one untimely born, he appeared also to me' (*1 Cor. 15:4–8*). So let us not make any mistake as to what is involved if the divinity of the Lord Jesus is questioned. The whole of the New Testament would need to be rewritten; the whole of our church services would have to be rewritten; we would be men and women without hope.

What would the apostle Paul have gained by *thinking* that he had met the risen Christ on the road to Damascus? In fact, humanly speaking, he did not gain anything, he lost by it. Instead of being honoured as a Jewish scholar he was now prepared to live without a home, without any of the comforts of life, to be persecuted and beaten, to be hated and hunted by his own people, and finally to be executed because he could not deny that Jesus Christ was God. He persisted in saying that through Jesus Christ he had entered into the realm of God. It is only if you accept this spiritually that you can account for the change in the life of the apostle. If Christ was not divine, Paul's life was meaningless and his writings were misleading documents, for in all of them he proclaimed Christ as Lord and Saviour – God manifest in the flesh. Unless this is true we are left with a human being of surpassing goodness but with no Saviour, and no hope for us. This is what Paul saw so clearly: 'But if there is no resurrection of the dead, then Christ has not been raised; if Christ has not been raised, then our preaching is in vain and your faith is in vain. We are even found to be misrepresenting God, because we testified of God that he raised Christ, whom he did not raise if it is true that the dead are not raised. For if the dead are not raised, then Christ has not been raised. If Christ has not been raised, your faith is futile and you are still in your sins. Then those also who have fallen asleep in Christ have perished. If for this life only we have hoped in Christ, we are of all men most to be pitied' (*1 Cor. 15:13–19*).

But thank God, Christ is alive and risen and working in this world through His grace. The apostle was telling these Philippian people, as he is telling you and me too, that in the experience on the Damascus road he met with Christ Himself – he came to know God in a way he had never known Him before. It was through Jesus Christ that he had found acceptance with God, access into His presence through His atoning death. It was through Jesus Christ that he had come into the relationship of sonship to God whereby he could call God his Father; it was through Jesus Christ that he had found eternal life. These things were beyond his greatest expectations, more than all the values of this world – his position and possessions or anything in the realm of scholarship that he might have had. He said 'For to me to live is Christ' because through Christ he had entered into this inheritance which transcended everything of this world. It was all a result of what happened on that day when he met Jesus Christ his Lord. Can you imagine this Jew, who was so concerned about the almighty God, ever using the word 'Lord' unless he believed that Jesus Christ *was* God? He said, '*All* have sinned and come short of the glory of God', but the One whom he met on the Damascus road was Jesus Christ. This is what the New Testament and Christianity are all about – that 'whosoever believeth in him should not perish but have everlasting life' (*John 3:16*). It is odious to compare the opinions of these theologians with the experience of Paul – they do not come near him in genius, service to God, in holiness or spirituality. It is worth reminding ourselves that this Jewish genius who had *hated* Christ was converted because the risen Christ broke into his life unasked. He told him, 'I am Jesus whom you are persecuting.' So many of the great saints of the church of God repeat the same realization of Christ as the risen Son of God – Augustine, Luther, Calvin, Wesley, Simeon, the great hymn-writers, and millions of men, women, and even children, who, through this experience, have found the peace of God and the forgiveness of God in Jesus Christ.

THE GRACE OF CHRIST

What does Paul mean by the 'grace of the Lord Jesus Christ'? I think it is vitally important for us to understand this because it is at the heart of his experience. Indeed, all the Pauline epistles can be scrapped if there is not such an experience as the grace of Christ, because it relates to what is either the greatest and most wonderful truth in the world or the greatest and most evil deception of sinful men. Because it is so vital for us to grasp the meaning of this word 'grace', let us look again at the Damascus road, for this is where Paul learned its true meaning.

Did the apostle deserve God's blessing as he travelled on

that road? *He* was the man who had hated and fought the Lord Jesus and all that He had taught and done. He had killed the children of God, hailing men, women and children and putting them into prison, smothering the Christians who had authority to continue this work, and he was on his way to decimate the church at Damascus. He had heard Stephen preaching – the call to repent, the evidence of the resurrection – the theology, if you like, behind the great address of Stephen to the council. He had seen Stephen die, and yet *he would not give in*! He was in a state of absolute unbelief and complete rejection of the gospel of Jesus Christ. From God's standpoint there was no reason why He should bless him; there was no merit in his standing before God, no grounds to expect forgiveness and eternal life by his mistaken efforts. God had come with something greater and more wonderful than He had done before; Jesus Christ was the fulfilment of all the Old Testament types, and Paul had misunderstood it all! But God *did* bless him: Jesus Christ met him, spoke to him, convinced him, captured and converted him; he was forgiven and reconciled to God for time and for eternity. It was a free gift from God, the gift of eternal life on account of the death of Jesus Christ. 'They are justified by his grace as a gift, through the redemption which is in Christ Jesus' (*Rom. 3:24*). It was the reverse of what he deserved; it was an unmerited gift of God, not given because of his obedience nor because of anything he had done. In fact, he had done so much to deserve the opposite, namely, to be condemned and separated from God because he had rejected His Son and His message; he had rejected the preaching and testimony of Stephen and the apostles. Why did God meet him? *The answer lies in the heart of God*. It was bestowed as a free gift and the word for this action of God is *grace* – the unmerited favour of God. Paul could never have spoken of grace in this way if it had been offered to him by a man; such an idea would be foreign to the New Testament; it would overthrow God's wonderful plan of salvation whereby, on account of His Son Jesus Christ, who died for our sins and rose again for our justification, God freely forgives us and acts towards us in grace.

THE RATIONALE OF THIS PRAYER

Why did Paul express this prayer for grace for the Philippian Christians? It was because grace includes the whole plan and means of salvation brought about by God. As Christians we all stand where the apostle stood – in the unmerited favour of God who, for His own reasons, according to His own counsel, and in His own sovereign grace, has broken into our lives too. We do not deserve to be forgiven; we have never earned eternal life; God freely forgives us. This is the great freedom of the gospel and people will not even listen to it. It is something so wonderful that we cannot really take it in. God *freely* forgives us. This is precisely what happened to Paul on the Damascus road, and if you only stop to meditate upon this experience you can see it clearly. Here was the persecutor of Jesus Christ being met by Him, freely forgiven by Him, restored and brought into a new relationship with Jesus Christ. This is where we stand too – every Christian stands here before God. So the apostle prayed this for the Philippian Christians because he wanted to remind them for ever that *everything that comes to us from God comes through grace*, and the grace of God comes to us only through Jesus Christ. It is grace that brings the personal application of the love of God to individuals and if the grace of God is rejected, then we have no hope. We are forgiven as a gift because Jesus Christ died for us on the cross; we have regained righteousness in the presence of God because we have been clothed with His righteousness. We have access into the presence of God because that access was gained for us through Jesus Christ. Because Jesus Christ gave Himself on the cross His

Spirit indwells us so that we may be the children of God. The apostle told the Philippians that *this* was the realm in which he wanted them to live – 'The grace of the Lord Jesus Christ be with your spirit.'

Moreover, it is the grace of the Lord Jesus Christ which changes us to become like Him, and ultimately it will be His grace which will enable us to be like Him absolutely and completely because when we see Him we shall be as He is. 'Now we see through a glass, darkly; but then face to face', and when we see Him we shall be like Him. Our song in heaven will be of the grace of the Lord Jesus Christ because it is through Him that God's love has come to us.

I want to remind you again of this great and wonderful foundation truth of our Christian faith, namely that the Lord Jesus Christ, God Himself, came into this world. God Himself dealt with our sin; He dealt with that which separated us from Himself. It was God who reconciled us to Himself through Jesus Christ. So Paul's prayer was that the Philippians – and *all* Christians – should live in the light and joy and wonder of the grace of the Lord Jesus Christ on account of whose death and resurrection the grace of God is poured out upon us. This is why the apostle said: 'The grace of the Lord Jesus Christ be with your spirit.'